T0195785

COOL for SCHOOL

A Guide to Ensuring Your Child's
Success in School.

Sheena Hendon

BALBOA.PRESS

A DIVISION OF HAY HOUSE

Balboa Press books may be ordered through booksellers or by contacting:

Balboa Press
A Division of Hay House
1663 Liberty Drive
Bloomington, IN 47403
www.balboapress.com
1 (877) 407-4847

Because of the dynamic nature of the Internet, any web addresses or links contained in
this book may have changed since publication and may no longer be valid. The views
expressed in this work are solely those of the author and do not necessarily reflect the
views of the publisher, and the publisher hereby disclaims any responsibility for them.

The author of this book does not dispense medical advice or prescribe the use
of any technique as a form of treatment for physical, emotional, or medical
problems without the advice of a physician, either directly or indirectly. The
intent of the author is only to offer information of a general nature to help you
in your quest for emotional and spiritual well-being. In the event you use any
of the information in this book for yourself, which is your constitutional right,
the author and the publisher assume no responsibility for your actions.

Print information available on the last page.

ISBN: 978-1-9822-4089-9 (sc)
ISBN: 978-1-9822-4091-2 (hc)
ISBN: 978-1-9822-4090-5 (e)

Library of Congress Control Number: 2020900322

Balboa Press rev. date: 01/13/2020

For Andrew, Dylan, and James with buckets of love.

CONTENTS

HOW IT ALL STARTED

A few years ago, I was chatting to a neighbour when the subject came up about whether her child, a four-year-old, was ready to start school.

"You're a naturopath and a nutritionist," she said. "Would you be willing to come and talk to our play centre about getting our kids ready for school? We want to find out about things like how to prepare them emotionally for their first day, what to put in their lunchbox, looking after their health naturally, and how to get them in tip-top condition before they start."

I said I would love to. I rocked up to the venue a few weeks later expecting a group of five or so parents. To find to my amazement, forty people had turned up! Forty caregivers were eager and enthused about giving their children the best start in life.

The concept of *Cool for School* was born.

Since that time, I have witnessed more and more parents, just like you, wanting to take control of their children's well-being as you become aware of the significant impact that our food, environment, medications, emotions, and even our DNA can have on the health of family members. And you, the caregivers, recognize that real control means understanding the science and research behind the health advice given. You seek to learn more about how to prevent as well as treat health issues without pharmaceutical intervention wherever possible, understand what foods your kids need to flourish and thrive and beat the obesity epidemic, and how to reduce digital toxicity and more.

And that is why I decided to write this book. It provides a practical guide to optimizing your children's health and wellness, naturally, to ensure they are happy, healthy, and thriving in their first years at school.

I created *Cool for School* from insight I gained through professional experiences working with families and individuals, and through talks and workshops. I combined this insight with the knowledge, joys, and tribulations I gained from raising two boys, as well as heaps of input from patients, friends, and parents with young (and older) children. The book aims to arm you with the information and tools you need to have your child ready to start school at an optimal mental, emotional, and physical level while providing you with natural solutions to get things back in balance when needed.

All our children are different. Every single one has a gorgeous individual emerging character with differing academic, learning, creative, and sports abilities and unique challenges to overcome. *Cool for School* addresses these issues to enable your gifted, beautiful children to thrive as they enter the next stage of their lives.

When I started to write this book, I put my parent head on and thought about how it was best to structure the information. I decided to write it to allow time-strapped and tired caregivers to delve into chapters relevant to their children without having to read the whole book. However, I strongly recommend reading from cover to cover; you never know what pearls of wisdom might reveal themselves as gifts to you, your child, family, or community.

Enjoy.

Warmest wishes,

Sheena X

Chapter 1

GETTING STUFF SORTED BEFORE THE BIG DAY

The transition from preschool to elementary school is often daunting for our children. Some kids may be anxious about it, while others may still seem too young—socially, mentally, and physically. Of course, many will breeze on in and embrace school from day one.

Remember, our children are going to be bombarded with a whole heap of newness when they start—new friends, a structured environment, long days, lessons, and loads more kids in one space than what they experienced at preschool. All of this can tax their brains and their emotions. Imagine the challenges of moving to a new country—a new workplace, new colleagues, new neighbours, a strange language, new foods, different rules, and a new environment. Pretty overwhelming, right? Perhaps this comparison will highlight what our children experience on the first day of school.

Don't assume

Before the big day arrives, I suggest having a casual conversation with your wee one about starting school. Discuss how he or she is feeling. Talk about everything that might be worrisome and answer any lingering questions. Allow your child to speak without making any assumptions.

For example, some kids feel uncomfortable going to the toilet in a strange place, and may even wet or soil themselves. Others may be anxious about meeting new children or getting constipation or having diarrhea.

We often think that, if one of our children has sailed through school, our other children will as well. One mother told me that her youngest took her totally by surprise when he expressed concerns about being able to understand math. It turned out that he was worried that he would be expected to do the same sums his brother was doing even though his brother was four years older. By getting her child to voice his concerns, she was able to help him feel better about starting school.

ENROLLING YOUR CHILD AT SCHOOL

A child can start school in New Zealand anytime between the ages of five and six; most children start school when they turn five. Once a child turns six, he or she must be enrolled and must attend school every day. Children begin school at different times throughout the academic year depending on when their birthdays fall. Unlike other countries, New Zealand does not have set start dates. School-enrolment laws vary from country to country.

Remember, parents decide when their children start school. Parents who are concerned that their five-year-old is not ready for school—perhaps they feel that their child may not be prepared socially or mentally—should have a conversation with the school administrators or an early childhood teacher who knows their kid. The best decision may be to wait a year.

Parents should notify the school once they've made a decision in order to help them with their planning. Decide on a start date, and then arrange some visits with your child to the school to help the child get used to the school. In New Zealand, parents may not be able to enrol their child at just any school. A zoned school has the authority to restrict enrolment to families living in the area. A ballot may be required in order to attend a zoned school outside the zone area.

Documents for enrolling

Check with the school to find out what paperwork is required. These forms may include:

- An enrolment form

- Proof of age and citizenship (birth certificate or passport)

- Immunization certificates (*The Well Child Book*)

- The child's doctor's contact details and the child's medical information (allergies, medications, etc.)

- Any relevant legal documents (for example custody and access issues)

- Emergency contact details (and a backup contact, if possible)

BEING READY EMOTIONALLY

Feel the fear and do it anyway

After spending the last few months trying on his or her new school uniform—a few sizes too big, of course—the big day has arrived. The new school bag is packed with new pens, pencils, notebooks, and a lunch box. School is finally going to start.

Remember to get the camera out to record this momentous event. On the morning of the first day of school, children should take lots of deep breaths. After a good breakfast, it's time to go.

Before the first day of school, there are heaps of things to consider that will help the day run smoothly. Here are some tips for normalizing the first day of school:

- Discuss the upcoming day and let her know it is normal to feel anxious or worried.

- Most children have school visits before the actual start day. Let your child know what to expect and how long he will be there.

- Take a walk around the school as a family to enable the child to get used to the environment, including where the toilets are, if possible. Have a play in the playground on weekends, if allowed.

- Play school at home. Practice writing your child's name and playing with toys. Send her to school with a packed lunch.

- Go on an outing to buy the school uniform, stationery, and a new lunch box.

- Find other kids in the area who may already be in the child's class or starting at the same time. Consider arranging a playdate.

- Develop a plan with the child and remind him who's picking him up and where to meet every day once school has started.

BEING MENTALLY AND PHYSICALLY READY

Children who have already been through an early childhood education (ECE) system will have already learned many of the things that will help them be ready for school. Simple things, such as knowing how to go to the toilet unaccompanied, knowing how to get dressed, knowing how to put on shoes—thank goodness for Velcro—and being able to ask for help can make a big difference in their daily school life.

Building a child's confidence will help him or her thrive in an academic setting. Here are some steps to ensure a smooth and stress-free transition.

The four-year-old health and development check

In New Zealand, every four-year-old is entitled to a free health-and-development check, which is called the B4 School Check. The scheme is run by the government, and it is the eighth and final of the well-child checks for children ages six weeks up to five years old. I suggest having this check after a child's fourth birthday, leaving enough time to get any help needed before school he or she starts school.

A local B4 School Check provider will contact parents and book their child in for the forty- to sixty-minute consultation. Parents will be asked to fill in a behavioural and a developmental questionnaire, and the child's ECE teacher will also contribute to the behavioural section.

The B4 School Check is carried out by a nurse and ensures that the child is healthy and can learn well. This exam also includes a hearing test and a vision test. The check is done with parental consent, and it's an ideal opportunity to discover and discuss any perceived problems. Parents may be referred to appropriate health, education, or social services. At this time, parents are entirely within their rights to be referred to their preferred health professional, such as a naturopath.

For New Zealand parents, further information about the B4 School Check can be found on the New Zealand Ministry of Health web page. For parents outside of New Zealand, explore whether there is a similar plan available to children.

Expectations when starting school

It helps if children have some basic skills and knowledge before starting school. New school starters should have the following abilities:

- Children should know their name. They should be able to recognize their first name and surname when it is written down. They should be able to tell a teacher what the first letter of their first name is, and should be able to write it down.

- Children should be well on their way to learning the alphabet. Children should be able to begin and possibly end the alphabet. If there are fuzzy parts in the middle, sorting the out will come. They should be able to identify at least half of the letters of the alphabet when they are written down.

- Children should know basic colours. It's helpful for children to start school knowing the names of the colours: red, blue, orange, yellow, green, black, brown, pink, and purple.

- Children should know simple item names. This includes the names of things they would find in a home or at school, such as mat, tap, toilet, book, pencil, chair, table, door, floor, and so on. Children will also need to realize that there are many names for the same things, such as writing implements. For example, there are pencils, pens, crayons, felt-tip markers, and so on.

- Children should be able to use basic manners, which includes phrases like thank you; No, thank you; please; excuse me; and may I …

- Children should be used to sharing.

- Children should know right from wrong, such as it's not okay to shout at or hit others. They should know that it is only acceptable to treat other people the way they want to be treated. They should be familiar with the concepts of "use your words" and "gentle hands."

- Children should be toilet trained. When children reach school age, they must be out of nappies and using a toilet. They need to be able to wipe their derrieres.

The first-day checklist

Tick	Item Required
	Clothing Tip: If parents have more than one child, get a whole lot of labels printed with just a surname and a phone number. Using the same tags for each child will save money.
	Hat—broad-brimmed or with a neck flap
	Sunglasses and a case
	School clothes, including: • school shirt or T-shirt that covers the shoulders • shorts or skirt • summer sandals or sturdy filled-in shoes with straps • sweatshirt for chilly days The school may have a uniform, so it pays to find out where to purchase it. They may even run a school uniform shop that sells new and used items.
	Schoolbag (backpack)

	Bookbag
	Swimming or sports bag
	Togs/swimming costume, towel, and goggles
	Lunch box (plastic-free please)
	Drink bottle (ideally metal not plastic)
	Stationery: most schools will provide a list
	Pencil case
	Pencils, pens, rubber, ruler, pencil sharpener
	Stationery (books and paper as specified by the school)
	Other stuff
	Any medication needs: such as asthma inhalers or an EpiPen in case of anaphylaxis

Remember, most children have some reservations about school. It is our job to normalize their concerns and work with them to make these new experiences as exciting and fun as possible. That means putting in the hard yards and getting stuff sorted before they get to school to have them be as physically, mentally, and emotionally powerful as possible.

What's your child's map of the world?

In the behavioural science of neuro-linguistic programming (NLP—one of the tools I use to support my patients), we talk about an individual's perception of the world as their "map". NLP teaches that our mind-body (neuro) and what we say (language) all interact together to form our perceptions of the world, or maps (programming). Each person's map determines feelings and behaviour.

We mean that the way we sense the world is entirely different from the way others sense it. So children may relate to things differently than an adult because of their limited life experience. Sometimes we, as adults, are in danger of pushing our maps on to our kids or not stopping to think or ask how something appears to them. For example, anxious persons may expect their children to be nervous about starting school when, in fact, they are feeling excited. Or, say, people who are great at sports may expect their children to sail through physical education sessions even though the reality is that some children have two left feet, struggle to catch a ball, and begin to loath outdoor activity time.

In both cases, we need to *stop*, breathe, and ask ourselves: Is this me reflecting my map or perception onto my child, or am I understanding my kid's viewpoint? Then you can figure out why your child does certain things, and you can change your behaviour in a way that supports your child even more.

Chapter 2

KIDS COMMON HEALTH ISSUES AND WHAT TO DO ABOUT THEM

Over two thousand years ago, the Greek physician Herophilus wrote, "When health is absent, wisdom cannot reveal itself, art cannot manifest, strength cannot fight, wealth becomes useless, and intelligence cannot be applied." I have pinned this statement to my clinic wall. It is an excellent reminder that, whatever your age, if something is going on with your health—mentally, physically or emotionally—you are not going to reach your full potential, and that's a fact.

There are critical health issues that may hinder your child from thriving at school. Unfortunately, these issues are often undiagnosed, and your kid can suffer. For example, these include the child who seems in a dream world but has glue ear and cannot hear the teacher. Or the one who continually gets told off for getting out of his seat when, in fact, he can't see the board due to poor eyesight. Perhaps your kid is the picky eater who has no energy and does not focus or is the one with sinus congestion or constant cough and cold who seems to be permanently off school sick. The list goes on. Fortunately, we can usually treat these issues.

I will tell you a story about my son James as a case in point. James had just started primary school, and for some reason or other, he happened to mention that he sometimes saw two of everything. Amazed that this had not been picked up—by myself, other family members, or health professionals—I asked him how long this had been going on and why he had not mentioned it before. He said that he had been seeing double for a few years and had failed to say anything because he thought seeing double was normal! Once we knew there was an issue, we got his eyes tested, and his problem was sorted.

Of course, kids get sick; they pick up bugs and viruses all the time. The important thing is how quickly they bounce back. If they don't recover quickly, then that is a sure sign that something needs to be checked out, and what better time than to do this before they start school.

As I said at the beginning, your child may breeze through starting school, but don't assume that is the case. If you follow the advice given in this book, then your wee one is more likely to be the one that cruises.

Try this quick quiz to see if common health complaints may need to be sorted to help your child reach her full potential.

Common health complaint	Yes/No	What to do
Infections and immunity		**See page 14**
Frequent ear infections		
Glue ear		
Persistent or recurrent coughs and colds		
Frequent bronchitis or colds going to the chest		
Vaccination reactions		
Numerous antibiotic courses		
Frequent urinary tract infections		
Digestion dilemmas		**See page 35**
Diarrhoea		
Constipation		

Tummy pain		
Excessive flatulence		
Bloating		
Allergy or intolerance		**See page 50**
Asthma		
Eczema		
Glue ear		
Rhinitis		
Hay fever		
Sinusitis		
Eating challenges		**See page 77**
Picky or fussy eater		
Limited diet		
Overweight for their age		
Underweight for their age		
Little energy		
Eczema or other skin disorders		**See page 59**
Behavioural issues		**See page 139**
ADD/ADHD or other diagnosed disorder		
Insomnia		
Stress-anxiety		
Lack of focus		
Bed wetting		
Difficulty controlling emotions		
Difficulty interacting with other children		

If you answer yes to any of these issues, your child may find it tricky to thrive at school.

POWERING UP YOUR CHILD'S IMMUNE SYSTEM

No kid enjoys being unwell, so what can you do to protect your children from viruses, bacteria, and other bug exposure? Of course, colds and flu are a fact of life, and in fact, they are a natural way for your children to keep healthy throughout their adult life. The important thing is to ensure that the immune system is robust enough for your kids to fight the nasties and quickly bounce back as good as new. Let's find out what healthy habits we can adopt that will supercharge your child's immune system.

What is immunity?

Your immune system, which is made up of specialized cells, proteins, tissues, and organs, defends you against germs and microorganisms every day. In most cases, the immune system does a great job of keeping people healthy and preventing infections. But sometimes problems with the immune system can lead to illness and disease.

Signs that a child's immune system is not working as it should show up as frequent infections, allergies, and behavioural disorders. Our immune system is complicated, but if you can understand the basics, you will be more easily able to prevent or reduce the severity of infections and provide solutions to building and maintaining a robust fighter for life.

Immune system basics 101

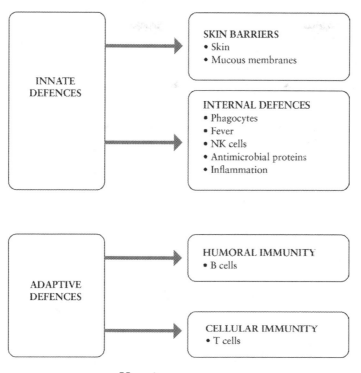

Your immune system

Your immune system is divided into two different types: innate immunity and adaptive immunity.

Innate immunity is something you are born with—it is already present in the body. As soon as something enters the skin, blood, or tissues, the immune system immediately goes into attack mode. It does this by identifying certain chemicals in the substance that tells the innate response it shouldn't be there. One example would be white blood cells fighting bacteria, causing redness and swelling when you have a cut.

Adaptive immunity is created in response to exposure to a foreign substance. When an alien invader such as a bacterial infection enters the body, the immune system takes it in and analyses its every detail.

Then the adaptive immune system responds by getting cells to attach to foreign substances every time they enter the body. The adaptive immune cells have a memory and know how to fight off specific invaders. One example is chickenpox—once we have had it, we are unlikely to get it again because our adaptive immune system has remembered the foreign body.

There is one more immunity type—**Passive immunity**. Passive immunity is "borrowed" from another source, and it lasts for a short time. For example, a baby gains temporary resistance to diseases due to antibodies in breast milk. These antibodies can help protect the baby against infection during the early years of childhood. So, wherever possible, and when it is the right thing for both mum and bub, I recommend that babies are breastfed up to at least six months.

Everyone's immune system is different. Some people never seem to get infections, whereas others appear to be sick all the time. People often become more immune to germs as they get older, which is why adults and teens tend to get fewer colds than kids; their bodies have learned to recognize and immediately attack many of the viruses that cause colds. That's why, when a child starts day care or school and is subjected to more bugs, they may seem to have a permanently ongoing infection. And if your immune system is also quite low, then you may start to pick up the germs they bring home and get sick more frequently.

Solutions for powering up immunity

Recurrent or chronic infections—even mild colds— occur only when the immune system is weakened. Thus, a vicious circle develops: a compromised immune system leads to infection, infection causes immune system damage, which further reduces resistance. Only by boosting the immune system can we break this cycle.

When it comes to your child's immunity, imagine it as a seesaw with the innate system on one end and the acquired at the other. At birth, the immune system of an infant is tipped high at the innate end—the innate system is in place, but the acquired immunity is not that established or strong yet. That is why children tend to have more allergies and more bacterial and viral infections (up to three a year is considered normal). If kids are frequently exposed to poor nutrition, lots of processed foods and chemicals, antibiotics, stress, and they haven't received breast milk, then immunity continues to be imbalanced. Optimum nutritional, dietary, and lifestyle habits are vital to bring the seesaw back into balance, enable the acquired immunity to take effect, and ensure an excellent immune system during their childhood and as an adult.

Ten ways to boost your kids' immunity

1. **Keep your kids dirty.** Yes, you heard correctly—interestingly, it's not in kids' interest to be too clean! I am sure many of you have heard of the "hygiene hypothesis." In brief, the hypothesis states that, over the past century, declining family size, improved household amenities, and higher standards of personal hygiene have reduced the opportunities for developing immunity and the rise in hay fever, asthma, and allergic diseases. When my kids were young, we bathed them only every other day or so, much to their delight. We let them play on the floor and didn't mind when they put their hands in their mouths. All of this encouraged a robust system. I suggest you do the same.

2. **Get to the guts of the problem—look after your microbiome.** Research suggests that a healthy gut, or more specifically, the microbiome, is vital to preventing illness and boosting immunity. The microbiome is a massive collection of trillions of microscopic organisms that live on and in your gut. Some of these microbes can cause infection and disease while

17

others help us keep in good health. The addition of beneficial probiotic bacteria can stop these baddies sticking to gut cells, inhibit their growth, and restore favourable microbial balance. Enhancing the growth of beneficial bacteria such as *Lactobacilli* and *Bifidobacterium* and slowing the activity of bacteria such as *Clostridium* and *Bacteroides* can get your child back on track.

Recurrent infections—bacterial, viral, fungal, or parasitic—are commonly treated with antibiotics, which can disrupt normal gut bacteria, which as we have said have loads of benefits including maintaining a healthy immune system. So, unfortunately, having imbalanced gut bugs tends to promote further infections and may start a vicious cycle.

If a child has had a course of antibiotics, I recommend that parents also give him high-strength probiotic capsules. They contain beneficial bacteria that live in the human digestive system and help the return of normal body functions after a course of antibiotics by reintroducing friendly bacteria into the colon to restore the gut flora. A probiotic from a health store or health care provider containing two strains of natural bacteria, *Lactobacillus rhamnosus* and *Lactobacillus acidophilus* is best. Take the probiotics two hours apart from the antibiotics to reduce the risk of the antibiotic preventing the probiotic from working.

As always, I recommend a varied and nutritious diet including a whole heap of microbiome-enhancing foods—garlic, lentils, whole grains, blueberries, and beetroot. See more about these in chapter 3.

3. **Keep antibiotics to the minimum.** Remember, antibiotics treat only illnesses caused by bacteria, but viruses cause most childhood illnesses. The simplest answer is to avoid

taking antibiotics altogether. Sometimes they are a necessary evil—the harm they do to your digestive system is more than balanced out by their lifesaving properties. However, make sure that, if your child is taking antibiotics, it is because she needs them. I strongly encourage parents to say to their doctor, 'Do you think it's necessary? Do you believe that we should swab to check it is a bacterium?'

4. **Be relaxed and happy.** There is growing research that documents the profound influence of the mind on physical disease. Mood and attitude have a tremendous bearing on immune system function. When we are stressed and emotionally upset, our immune system suffers. It's not only major life traumas that can depress immunity, but everyday stress has a significant impact. Stress increases the levels of adrenal hormones, including adrenaline. These hormones inhibit white blood cell formation and function and cause the thymus gland (where immune cells called T lymphocytes, are produced) to shrink, suppressing the immune function and leaving the individual vulnerable to infections, cancer, and other illnesses.

   What could be stressing your child? Even the act of starting school can cause anxiety, as can bullying or upsets at home—from parental arguments to moving to a new house. Start to notice whether stress or anxiety is big in your child's life and check out solutions in chapter 6.

5. **Get enough Zzzzs.** Research indicates that sleep deprivation can make us more susceptible to illness by reducing natural killer cells, immune-system weapons that attack microbes and cancer cells. Children in day care may be particularly at risk for sleep deprivation because all the activity and noise can make it difficult for them to nap. How much sleep do kids need? A newborn may need up to eighteen hours of a day.

toddlers require twelve to thirteen hours, and preschoolers and school starters need about ten hours.

6. **Eat more fruits and veggies.** Blackcurrants and berries, carrots, green beans, oranges, and lemons all contain immunity-boosting phytonutrients like vitamin C, polyphenols, and carotenoids. Phytonutrients may increase the body's production of infection-fighting white blood cells and interferon, an antibody that coats cell surfaces, blocking out viruses. Get your child to eat five servings of seasonal fruits and veggies a day in lots of different colours and varieties.

7. **Stop smoking around your kids.** Cigarette smoke contains a horrendous 4,000 or more toxins, most of which can irritate or kill cells in the body. Our children are more susceptible than adults to the harmful effects of second-hand smoke because they breathe at a faster rate; a child's natural detoxification system is also less developed. Second-hand smoke increases a child's risk of sudden infant death syndrome (SIDS), bronchitis, ear infections, and asthma and may also affect intelligence and neurological development. If you absolutely can't quit smoking, you can reduce your child's health risks considerably by smoking outside.

8. **Consider nutraceuticals and herbs.** Sometimes it helps to give the system a boost by taking an immune-enhancing nutritional supplement including vitamins and minerals such as vitamins A, C, E, selenium, and zinc. Herbs that are immune modulating and antimicrobial (fight the baddies)— echinacea, golden seal, St John's wort, thyme, oregano, pelargonium, eyebright, and garlic to name but a few—may also be useful. I love herbs as they are often critical in getting a biological shift in the body. However, to ensure you are

prescribed herbs suitable and safe for your child, do visit a qualified medical herbalist.

9. **Try pure essential oils.** Pure essential oils are also a fabulous and safe option for children. Those that address immunity and infection issues include oregano, melaleuca, rosemary, and eucalyptus. I have had great results with ear, nose, and throat infections using only essential oils externally. So, if your child has glue ear and maybe heading for grommets, contact your natural health professional to discuss what options may be available for your child.

10. **Get moving as a family.** Finally, research shows that exercise increases the number of bug-fighting natural killer cells, in adults, and regular activity can benefit kids in the same way. To get your children into a lifelong fitness habit, be a good role model and exercise with them rather than urging them to go outside and play. Fun family activities include bike riding, hiking (make it an adventure), basketball, cricket on the beach, and tennis.

Beating the Superbugs

First, what is a superbug? It's a term we use to describe bacteria that cannot be killed using multiple antibiotics. Taking antibiotics when you don't need them, or not finishing all your medicine, are factors contributing to this problem. Any bacteria species can turn into a superbug.

Here's how that might happen. When properly used, antibiotics can help destroy disease-causing bacteria. But if you are prescribed and take an antibiotic when you have a viral infection that's causing, for example, a sore throat, the drug won't make you better; instead, it may destroy a wide variety of bacteria in your body, including some of the "good" bacteria that help you fight infection, digest food, and keep well. Bacteria that are robust enough to survive the antibiotic may grow and quickly multiply. These drug-resistant strains may even spread to other people.

One superbug you may have heard of is methicillin-resistant *Staphylococcus aureus* (MRSA), which can cause skin infections, pneumonia, or bloodstream infections. The scary thing is that, if we continue to overuse antibiotics, then drug-resistant bacteria may continue to thrive, grow, and spread and share their drug-resistant characteristics with other bacteria, which will become more and more prevalent so that anyone can become infected.

You can help by taking antibiotics only when needed. For example, many ear infections get better without antibiotics, so don't insist on an antibiotic. It's best to delay if possible and check out the ways to fight infections naturally, as outlined in this book.

What about vaccinations?

As a parent, it is up to you to make an informed choice of whether to vaccinate or not. Some children have adverse effects to vaccinations, which are often due to an underlying immune balance. To prevent or minimize reactions, follow my guidelines above to make sure your precious ones have a robust, healthy immune system through proper nutrition, a great home environment, and minimal stress and anxiety.

Knowing how to read lab test results

I will often send patients to get laboratory tests done, such as blood or stool analyses (or I'll ask them to bring me the results of tests requested by their GP or specialist), as they can be a useful part of the picture to help pinpoint what may be going on.

I mention this because it's surprising how many people do not request a copy of the tests for their records; neither do they understand how to read them.

My suggestion is that you always request a copy of the tests to be sent to you. In New Zealand, this is easy to do, and there is no cost. It's good to have copies of all your tests if you change health provider. Additionally, you have some past records to compare with recent tests. Understanding these test results helps you take some control of the health of you and your family.

Don't worry; you don't need to be a rocket scientist to read blood tests, and you are not expected to understand the results entirely. Firstly, start by noticing where your reading sits. Is it in the middle of the reference range (the average) or near the minimum or maximum figure? If it is nearer the maximum or minimum value, you can discuss the result with your doctor or other health professional.

Be aware that your doctor has many tests to look at and may be alerted only to tests that show results that are outside the range. As an example, let's say the range of one marker is 20 to 50 and your test result shows 21. Your doctor may not see the result because the reading does not have an H for high or an L for low next to it. Your neighbour gets the same test done with a reading of 19, which means the GP is alerted and takes a different course of action.

Laboratory tests can help diagnose many health conditions. However, don't be alarmed about one abnormal blood test. Talk it through with your health professional to see what, if anything, needs to happen next.

Sheena's Words of Wisdom: Fever Phobia

Many parents have what I call fever phobia—a fear of febrile seizures (convulsions that can occur during a fever that affect kids three months to six years old). These seizures are usually accompanied by a temperature above about 38°C and last for a few minutes.

We must remember that fever is usually beneficial and an important immune defence mechanism. The simple act of raising of body temperature during fever kills many microorganisms and stops the viruses and bacteria replicating.

Fever management, therefore, should focus on keeping the child comfortable.

Managing a fever naturally

Monitor and allow the fever to run its natural course so that it's resolved as quickly as possible.

Only intervene if the temperature is over 38.3°C in an infant and 39°C in a child. Prevent dehydration with frequent sips of water.

If you need to reduce a fever, try YEP tea (an equal blend of yarrow, elderflower and peppermint tea). Use 10 grams each of the following dried herbs:

- Yarrow (to bring down fever)

- Elderflower (to bring down fever)

- Peppermint (to bring down fever)

- Echinacea (for immune support)

- Chamomile (to calm a distressed child)

Blend the dried herbs and use one teaspoon in a cup of boiling water. Infuse for ten minutes and ensure the tea has cooled. Give your child sips throughout the day and night when he is awake.

Do not use cooling or sponge baths or rub the body with alcohol or ice because these may increase the core body temperature. Lukewarm water sponging is okay.

Never use aspirin. Never use ibuprofen for infants less than six months. Never mix ibuprofen and paracetamol (acetaminophen). Use paracetamol first but only if the temperature stays too high for more than two hours in an infant or six hours in a child. Strengthen the immune system in the long term, as described in this chapter.

Case Study: Ear, Nose, and Throat Infections

Gorgeous, five-year-old Elly came to see me because her parents were concerned about the constant colds, ear infections, and bronchitis she had experienced over the past year. Not only was she having a lot of time off school—affecting her learning and friendships—but also the parent's work was often disrupted due to the time they needed to take off to look after her.

After questioning Elly's mum, I learned that Elly had been taking a lot of antibiotics in the past year to try to clear the infections. Additionally, her diet was high in sugar, and because she was a fussy eater, she hardly ate any vegetables or meat.

The treatment plan:

- **Treating the cause.** We worked to improve Elly's diet by slowly improving the amount of good-quality protein and vegetables to help increase her consumption of immune-supporting nutrients. We found that adding smoothies containing a combination of fruits and vegetables (upping the veggies and reducing the fruit gradually) such as berries and spinach, worked well. This incorporated vegetables she would usually not try, and it got her taste buds acclimatized to less-sweet flavours.

- Rather than "taking" sugar out of the diet, the emphasis was on swapping out sugary foods for more healthful ones or opting for low-sugar alternatives. I educated Mum and Elly on what foods were high in sugar.

- **Heal the gut and normalize gut bacteria.** We prescribed a gut-healing powder specifically for children containing glutamine, licorice, St Mary's thistle, and aloe vera as well as a probiotic powder containing several strains of bacteria *(Lactobacillus acidophilus, Bifidobacterium lactis,* and *Lactobacillus rhamnosus).* We added the powder to her smoothies. Additionally, we encouraged the addition of fermented foods to the diet in the form of plain, unsweetened probiotic yoghurt.

- **Support the immune system.** I am a great user of pure essential oils. To ensure Elly's ear infections cleared up entirely without antibiotics, I made some ear drops in a fractionated coconut oil base with melaleuca, lavender, and frankincense. This was rubbed around the ear (not in the ear). Additionally, we added a vitamin and zinc powder and liquid fish oil to the smoothie.

  We prescribed the supplements for six months, but some were gradually tapered off after a few months.

The results:

Elly's mum followed the regime to a T, and Elly quickly improved. It's been a year now. She has not had one ear infection, and her immune system seems robust.

The Last Word:

Even though it shouldn't surprise me, I often feel amazed out how simple it can be to get our health back on track without medication and with just a few nutrition and lifestyle tweaks and an initial boost with some nutraceuticals.

BREATHING EASY: COMMON RESPIRATORY INFECTIONS

The respiratory system focuses on the air we breathe. We know the symptoms of respiratory infections well—a snotty, runny nose; sore throat; red eyes; hoarseness; cough; temperature; and swollen lymph nodes. Kids are more prone to respiratory illnesses than adults, with up to six infections a year being the norm. That's because a child's respiratory tract does not fully develop until about six years of age. Additionally, as the breathing system is developing, so is the child's immune system.

Viruses cause most respiratory infections, which are contagious and spread from one person to another through respiratory droplets produced from sneezing and coughing. You may have noticed that, when your child started at a childcare centre or school, with a load of kids crawling all over each other, they seemed to catch more bugs.

Being able to prevent or treat these infections—the common cold, ear infections, sinusitis, tonsillitis, and bronchitis—at home and naturally is important for these reasons:

- As we found out earlier in the book, viruses cannot be treated with antibiotics.

- Many different viruses can cause colds and flu, and total immunization is not possible.

- Conventional over-the-counter medicine does not work well.

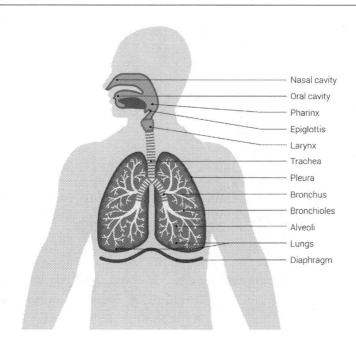

Nasal cavity
Oral cavity
Pharinx
Epiglottis
Larynx
Trachea
Pleura
Bronchus
Bronchioles
Alveoli
Lungs
Diaphragm

The Respiratory System
Human Body Systems

Your respiratory system

Treating respiratory infections

In this section, I will talk about the natural prevention and treatment of the most common infections colds, ear infections, sore throats, and tonsillitis. Next, we will find out how traditional cures, from lemon and honey drinks to steam inhalations and natural medicines, can make a big difference.

Before you read this section, I suggest that you check out "Powering Up Your Child's Immune System", and "Food Allergy or Intolerance? How Do You Know? These sections will give you more insight and confidence to manage your child's infection without having to visit your doctor to work out what to do. However, it is important to visit your preferred health care professional if you have any concerns about the state of your child's health.

The respiratory tract—all the parts of the body used in respiration— is made up of the upper airways including the nose, sinuses, throat, pharynx, larynx, and bronchi, and the lower airway including trachea, bronchi, and bronchioles.

The invasion of the lining (the mucous membrane) of the upper airway by a virus or bacteria can cause infections. But for these baddies to invade this membrane, they must fight through several physical and immunologic barriers. Hairs in the nose can trap invading bugs, wet mucus inside the nose can eat up the organisms, and small hair-like structures (cilia) that line the trachea move invaders up to the mouth to be swallowed and dealt with by our digestive system (doesn't that sound so disgusting!).

In addition to these physical barriers, the immune system also does its part to fight the invasion. Our adenoids and tonsils are a part of the immune system; natural antibodies and chemicals within them engulf and destroy invading microbes. But they sometimes become infected and even cause airway obstruction or repeated bacterial infections.

As you can see, we have an incredible defence system, but sometimes it just doesn't manage to keep the aliens out, particularly if your child is run down or has an immune system that is not working optimally.

A word about strep throat

Strep throat is an infection that results in an inflamed and sore throat caused by a group of bacteria called *Streptococcus*. Viruses, not strep bacteria, cause most sore throats, but if symptoms of a sore throat with a headache, fever, and upset stomach continue, then do get your child to a doctor for testing and antibiotics.

Strep throat can lead to the development of rheumatic fever, especially in children. Rheumatic fever affects the joints, heart, skin, and nervous system and may cause long-term damage to the heart and its valves.

The symptoms of respiratory infections usually last between three to fourteen days; if symptoms last longer than that, then your child may have sinusitis, an allergy, pneumonia, or bronchitis and should be checked out by a health professional.

What can we do to prevent or manage these infections naturally?

Adopt healthy habits to supercharge your child's immunity. Checkout "Ten Ways to Boost Your Kids' Immunity".

- Understand how allergies and intolerance may play a part.

- Encourage your child to wash her hands thoroughly and often to reduce the spread of bugs.

- Encourage lots of sleep and provide heaps of cuddles and love—a sure way to get the immune system back on track.

- Try gargling with lukewarm saltwater or using steam inhalations.

How to make saltwater gargle

Mix one teaspoon of salt into a cup of warm water. Your child may be too young to try this; most kids can gargle when they are six to eight years old

How to make and use a steam inhalation

I still remember doing this as a kid. It's easy to do and one the best remedies for coughs, colds, sinus infection, sore throats, and clearing chest mucus.

Pour boiling water into a large bowl. For kids, cool it down a bit so it is just hot (we don't want to run the risk of burning them with the steam). Have the child place his face over the bowl, and cover his head and the bowl with a large bath towel. Take care that the child's face is far enough away from the steam to avoid burns. Allow the child to inhale the hot steam for several minutes. For a cold, a persistent cough, or a sinus infection, steam inhalations can be done several times a day.

You can also make the inhalation more effective by adding three to four drops of essential oil to the water. Especially use those with anti-bacterial and antiviral or decongestant properties. Eucalyptus, pine, lavender, rosemary, peppermint and tea tree are fabulous oils to use.

Essential oils for steam inhalations

- Colds: Eucalyptus (*Eucalyptus globulus* or *radiata*) is antiviral, antibacterial, and decongestant. Or try lavender (*Lavandula angustifolia*), pine (*Pinus sylvestris*), tea tree (*Melaleuca alternifolia*), or peppermint (*Mentha piperita*).

- Coughs: Eucalyptus oil relieves congestion, and if there is an infection, it also fights the bacteria. For dry and irritating coughs, try frankincense (*Boswellia carterii*).

- Sinus infection: Try eucalyptus, lavender, peppermint, pine, thyme (*Thymus vulgaris*) or tea tree.

- A sore throat: Use lavender and thyme.

Safety Precautions

Steam inhalations aren't recommended for people with asthma, hay fever, and other similar allergies. If you have any concerns, don't use this treatment, or at least start with a short amount of time, just half a minute.

- An alternative to steam inhalation is to place a few drops of eucalyptus oil on a clean cloth and sniff it. It's a sure way to clear the nasal passages.

- If your child has a blocked-up nose from a cold, sinus problems, or allergies, nasal irrigation is the bee's knees.

How to do nasal irrigation

Start with one to two cups of boiled *warm* water. Add a quarter to a half teaspoon of non-iodized salt and a pinch of baking soda. Cool down the solution. You can buy saline solution nasal irrigation kits from your pharmacy if you prefer.

Then, have handy a squeezy bottle, neti pot, or syringe. Lean your child forward over the sink, at about a forty-five-degree angle. Tilt her head so that one nostril is pointed down toward the sink. Don't tilt her head back.

Now slowly squeeze the saltwater (saline) solution into one nostril. It will flow through the nasal passages, washing out mucus and allergens, and drain out of the other nostril and mouth. Tell your child to spit the water out and not to swallow it. It won't hurt if some go down her throat.

Get your child to blow her nose and do the same thing with the other nostril.

Don't use this treatment if the child has an ear infection or a bunged-up nose that's hard to breathe through.

Other natural treatments

- Lemon and honey in warm water is a lovely way to boost your child's immune-busting vitamin C levels and soothe a sore throat or tonsillitis. Add the juice of a lemon and a teaspoon of honey to a cup of warm water and sip.

- If you are brave, you can try your child on a teaspoon of chopped up antioxidant, immune-strengthening raw garlic, onion, and ginger to beat the bugs. You may have better luck than I ever had. I could never persuade my boys to try it, but I reckon that the threat of a dose of this concoction got them back to school a lot faster! That and turning off the wifi.

- Middle ear infections (otitis media) can be treated successfully with essential oils too. Never put oils directly into the ear. Apply one to two drops of tea tree, lavender, frankincense, or On Guard® (an oil manufactured by DōTERRA) on the surface of the ear and behind the ear. Also, apply a drop of oil on a small cotton ball and place over the ear opening (do not press it into the ear canal).

- A whole heap of herbs can be useful with respiratory illnesses:

  o Expectorants (pelargonium) to remove secretions from the lungs

  o Demulcents (marshmallow root or leaves) to soothe and reduce inflammation

  o Spasmolytics (elecampane, thyme, and liquorice) to relax the bronchioles

  o Anticatarrhals (eyebright, elderflower, and mullein) to get rid of discharge and reduce congestion.

  o Antiseptics (pelargonium and garlic) to fight infection.

o Antitussives which include the anticatarrhal, demulcents, and expectorants and may reduce a cough and soothe irritation

o Antiallergic (albizzia and baical skullcap)

o Mucolytics (garlic and horseradish) to relieve congestion

- Depending on your child's appetite, foods such as chicken soup and bone broth as well as high-vitamin C fruits and juices (blackcurrants and citrus) are ideal for keeping up your child's energy and strength to fight the infection. It may be worth avoiding mucus-forming foods such as dairy, or hot spicy foods that can be irritating and all processed foods. Keep serving sizes small to make the food more appealing.

- Keep up fluid consumption. Lemon and honey or blackcurrant drinks, weak herbal teas, and water are best.

Sheena's Words of Wisdom: Prevention vs Cure

I am going to start sounding like a broken record, but I'll say it again: prevention is better than cure. If you look after your children's health and wellness following the diet and lifestyle suggestions I offer in later chapters, they will, usually, get sick less often and bounce back from the lurgy much faster.

GETTING TO THE GUTS OF DIGESTIVE PROBLEMS

All diseases begin in the gut.

—Hippocrates, 460–370 BC

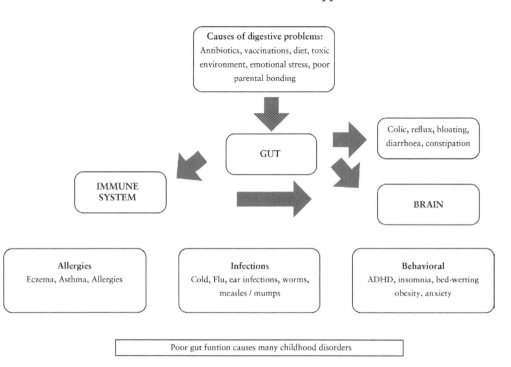

Causes and symptoms of digestive problems

Many health professionals, including myself, would agree that a child's digestive system is the route of all health, and this thinking is backed up by evidence-based research. When a child's digestive system is under functioning, it can cause issues such as poor appetite, bloating, flatulence, abdominal pain, and food intolerances. It can also have a direct effect on the immune system, showing up as eczema, asthma, allergies, colds and flu, ear infections, or worms. Additionally, it seems that tummy troubles may also influence brain development leading to behavioural dysfunction and symptoms such as attention-deficit disorder (ADD) and attention-deficit/ hyperactivity disorder (ADHD), insomnia, bed-wetting, anxiety, and is also linked to obesity.

If the tummy is irritated, inflamed, or constipated, it can't do its job, and your child's health can be at risk. The great news is that there are natural ways to help resolve your child's digestive complaints.

Seven top reasons why a healthy tummy is important

1. Our gut is where we digest and absorb the nutrients from the foods we eat. If digestion is working well, we can use all the goodness in the food we eat to provide the nutrition for every cell in our body. Excellent absorption leads to optimal health, including great brain function and energy levels.

2. Are you aware that the gut is the biggest immune organ in the body? It produces more antibodies than any other body system and contains most of our antibody-producing cells. The healthy bacteria in our tummies act as the first line of defence against pathogens (baddies) that we may ingest. A healthy microflora can also reduce the incidence of allergies with their immune-regulating action. A belly full of "good" bacteria is integral to a robust immune system.

3. Healthy gut flora will ensure the functioning of gut-associated lymphoid tissue (GALT), the largest immune organ of the body, and found in the gut lining. Without the healthy gut flora that colonizes GALT, the gut will not operate at full capacity.

4. Gut microflora also play a role in behavioural disorders such as autistic spectrum disorders. Children with these behavioural disorders tend to have some form of a gastrointestinal problem. It seems that disruption of the microbiome (the soup of bacteria, fungi, and viruses that live naturally in our

digestive tract) may lead to problems with the nervous system, influencing behaviour.

5. Imbalances in the microflora may cause inflammation that may disrupt the production of brain chemicals such as serotonin. These brain chemicals play a role in our children's behaviours, moods, sleep patterns, and energy levels.

6. A healthy gut produces enzymes needed to assist with the breakdown of our food.

7. Gut lining inflammation, low stomach acid, and an imbalance in good and bad gut microflora can contribute to the development of eczema and other skin conditions

Signs and symptoms that might indicate your child may have a gut imbalance

- Irritable bowel syndrome (IBS) or problems with digestion: complaints of abdominal pain, flatulence, a firm and bloated stomach, or changeable stools such as diarrhoea to constipation or straining

- Allergies and food intolerances

- Nausea and poor appetite

- Mood changes: hyperactivity, anger, irritability, or sadness

- Skin conditions such as eczema or other rashes or spots

- Depression, anxiety, and associated symptoms such as bedwetting

- Low energy and fatigue

- Learning difficulties, inability to concentrate, and irritability

What causes poor gut function?

Many factors can disrupt or disturb a child's digestive system. These may include a nonvaginal birth, lack of breastfeeding, vaccinations, poor diet, food intolerances, emotional sensitivity or stress, weak parental bonding, and the environment in which the child lives. Let's look at all these factors in more detail.

- **Vaginal microbes**. Babies' microbiomes (the microorganisms that collect around the body) have a significant influence on their overall health. Vaginal secretions provide a new-born with a starter pack of microbes that may sculpt his immune system in ways that combat disorders including obesity, asthma, and allergies. Interestingly, it may become the norm for babies born via C-section to be wiped down with their mother bacteria-laden vaginal fluid.

- **Breastfeeding.** As well as an excellent source of nutrition, breast milk plays a vital role in the transfer of mum's immune system, including health-promoting bacteria, to the baby. Also, her breast milk contains unique sugars that seem to nourish the gut bacteria that infants need.

- **Dysbiosis:** Did you know that there are more bacteria in the gastrointestinal tract than there are cells in the whole of our body? Also, there are about 400 to 1,000 different species of these bacteria—both good and bad—that live together as the gut microbiome, as I discussed earlier in this chapter. Symbiosis (which translates to "living in harmony") occurs when our intestines contain a balance of good and bad bacteria that lead to good health.

Dysbiosis is the opposite; it's when the bad guys take over and there is an imbalance of microbial colonies. The problem is that the good guys are vital. They help with digestion and absorption. They produce vitamins and control the growth of harmful microorganisms. Dysbiosis, which can result from not enough good bacteria or an overgrowth of harmful organisms such as yeasts (candida), parasites, and harmful bacteria, can lead to illness and disease.

- **Small intestinal bacterial overgrowth (SIBO).** Methane or hydrogen-producing bacteria in the small intestine causes abdominal pain, discomfort, excess gas and bloating, and abnormal bowel motions. The cause may include use of proton pump inhibitors, a gastro bug, and poor gut mobility (for example because of constipation or even stress).

- **Poor diet:** Research shows that diets high in sugar may harm the structure and function of the microbiota. While there's no need to eliminate sugars completely. The World Health Organization (WHO) recommends that no more than 10 per cent of calories should come from added sugars. Added sugars include glucose, fructose, and sucrose added to food and drink, or naturally occurring sugars in refined foods such as honey, coconut sugar, or fruit juice.

- **Intolerances or sensitivities:** A high number of kids have food sensitivities, which can cause symptoms such as bloating, flatulence, constipation, and diarrhoea. More on allergy and intolerance later.

- **Stress and anxiety:** A heap of research indicates that the gut is vulnerable to long- and short-term stress and anxiety. Studies have demonstrated changes in gut secretions and motility, gut wall permeability, barrier function, and blood flow as well as a lower threshold for abdominal pain. Evidence also suggests that stress signals lead to changes in the types of microorganisms living in the gut.

We can rebuild our kids' digestive health

What can you do to improve the health of your children's gut?

- **Sort out their nutrition.** Provide a varied, balanced diet with a heap of fruit and vegetables, lean meats, fish, nuts, pulses, legumes, and lashings of fish or flax oil. Cut down on those takeaways and sweet biscuits, cakes, and soft drinks. Encourage your wee ones to drink loads of water throughout the day (between rather than with meals, as water dilutes the stomach acid and slows down digestion). Also encourage them to chew their food well. Unsweetened acidophilus yoghurt is also perfect for the gut.

  Fermented foods such as kefir, kombucha, kimchi, miso, and sauerkraut even in small amounts are also worth considering. They are full of probiotics, which feed healthy bacteria. Some of you may be saying, "My kid won't eat these!" Give it a go. You may be surprised.

- **Add a variety of microbiome-enhancing foods.** These foods are what we call prebiotics: inulin, fructo-oligosaccharides (FOS), galacto-oligosaccharides (GOS), and lactulose, as well as prebiotic-like compounds like resistant starch, pectins, whole grains, polyphenols, and fibre. These foods provide a packed lunch for our gut microbes allowing them to flourish.

Examples of microbiome enhancing foods your kids will love:

FOS and Inulin	Resistant starch	Fibre	Polyphenols	Other prebiotic foods
Asparagus, bananas Barley, garlic, Honey Leeks Onions Tomatoes Rye	Roasted or steamed, cooled potatoes Bananas Cashew nuts Uncooked rolled oats White beans Lentils, cooked	Flax seeds Hemp seeds Vegetables Fruit Whole grains	Blueberries Strawberries Peaches Plums Grapeseed extract Tea Cocoa Chocolate (dark)	Kiwi fruit Beetroot Green peas Snow peas Sweetcorn Kidney beans Watermelon Dried fruits (apricots, dates, figs)

- **Boost dietary fibre.** Eating adequate dietary fibre plays a critical role in gut health, including feeding and cultivating healthy bacteria. Your child will get enough fibre if she is eating at least five servings of fruits and vegetables each day as well as other fibre-rich foods. Some of the best sources of dietary fibre include fruits (with skin on where appropriate), vegetables (especially dark green ones), beans (legumes), starchy vegetables (like pumpkin and parsnips), whole grains, and psyllium and flax.

- **Explore allergies and intolerances.** Food sensitivities and gut health can become a vicious cycle: poor nutrition may lead to an inflamed gut, which can then cause food problems. This subject is delved into in more detail later in the chapter. However, a trial diet that omits a suspect food or food group such as the FODMAP diet (fermentable oligosaccharides, disaccharides, monosaccharides and polyols) for IBS relief, gluten or dairy-free elimination diets, and so forth will give the intestinal tract a holiday and a chance to heal. A word of warning: eliminating food groups for an extended period can be detrimental to your child unless you know what you are doing. Hence, elimination diets must be carried out under the supervision of a qualified health professional.

- **Encourage regular daily activity.** See chapter 5.

- **Om!** Find a way to identify any stresses in your child's life and work to remove them. See chapter 6.

- **Give nutraceuticals a go.** Well-known gut healers include probiotics such as acidophilus, glutamine, aloe vera, magnesium, digestive enzymes, fibre powders such as psyllium, and herbs such as ginger, gentian, chamomile, and wormwood.

Of course, each kid will have different health causes and symptoms. It might pay to visit a dietitian, nutritionist, naturopath, or doctor to sort things out and to get tested for intestinal parasites and food allergies or sensitivities.

Sheena's Words of Wisdom: Make Life Choices for Good Digestive Health

In most cases, digestive problems stem from lifestyle choices. Diet, emotions, and activity level can each play a big part in the cause.

By tweaking these components, not only will our kids stop having tummy problems, but changes will play a significant role in reducing the incidence of lifestyle diseases, from heart disease and diabetes to obesity and auto-immune conditions later in life. As we know, prevention is better than cure!

WHAT'S AT THE BOTTOM OF CONSTIPATION

As so many kids seem to have constipation these days, I felt that a whole section on the subject was warranted. To me, long-term constipation is a clear symptom that something is not right with the child. The condition can be distressing and embarrassing for your school starter; it should be addressed as soon as possible.

What is it?

Your child has constipation if he has a hard poo or does not empty his bowel regularly.

What are the signs and symptoms?

- Your child's poo is hard, small, and pebble-like, or your child regularly has not had a poo for four days or so.

- There may be soiling incidents.

- Your child is in pain or is upset when having a poo.

- Your child complains of tummy pain that goes away when passing faeces.

- Your child may have urine incontinence, frequent urinary tract infections, or may wet the bed—all of which may increase if your child is constipated.

What causes it?

Constipation in children is common and is often due to a combination of factors:

- A natural tendency to have a more sluggish gut, which means that food passes slowly through the digestive tract, and constipation is more likely.

- A poor diet high in animal fat (fatty meat and dairy products) and refined sugar (rich desserts, sugary drinks, and other sweets), and low in fibre (vegetables, fruits, whole grains). There is little roughage in most convenience or "junk" food.

- Less activity and not eating and drinking, such as when your child is sick.

- Not drinking enough fluids.

- Bowel habits. Your child can become constipated if she ignores the urge to have a poo or fails to empty her bowel fully when she goes to the toilet.

How a vicious cycle is established

Constipation often starts after one hard poo has caused pain. The natural response to a painful experience is to try and avoid or escape it in the future. Therefore, the next time the child feels the urge to go, he holds on to avoid pain. As the stool becomes firmer and larger and even more painful to pass, the child becomes even more reluctant to go. In this way, a vicious cycle is established: Hard poo—pain—try to avoid pain by "holding on" to poo—hard poo—pain—and so on.

What if constipation continues for a long time?

If constipation continues for a long time, and the bowel isn't emptied regularly, the bowel becomes overloaded and stretches. This causes the sensation to pass a stool to be lost, which can make soiling accidents more likely.

Could childhood constipation be due to an abnormal bowel?

Constipation is hardly ever due to an abnormal bowel. Most anatomical bowel problems show up in early life and are diagnosed within the first few months. If your child passed meconium (the green/ black poo passed by new-born babies) within twenty-four hours of birth, it is unlikely your child has a bowel problem that is causing constipation.

What can be done to treat it?

Try simple measures first:

- Increase your kid's daily water intake. Ensure she has a good drink every few hours and extra fluid when it's hot.

- Increase fruit and vegetables in your child's diet, as the fibre makes the poo softer and easier to pass. Giving your child (if aged over fifteen months old) more fibre can help prevent constipation and treat short-term, mild constipation.

- Include probiotic foods such as plain probiotic yoghurt, sauerkraut, kefir, kombucha or coconut water may help bowel function.

How to up the fibre

- Serve cereals high in fibre such as bran flakes, wholemeal Weet-Bix, and whole-grain cereals and porridge. Avoid those that are refined such as cornflakes, rice bubbles, or those with added sugar. Serve wholemeal bread instead of white bread (except in children under fifteen months old). Add bran to muffins, other baked goods or cereal, or add ground flaxseed and hempseed to yoghurt, stewed fruit, cereals, soup, and smoothies.

- Include at least three servings of fruits each day; fruits with the peel left on, (apples, plums, prunes, apricots, and peaches) have a lot of fibre as do kiwi fruit and berry fruit.

- Include at least three servings of vegetables each day; this includes potato, kumara (also known as sweet potatoes, and do leave the skin on), and pumpkin.

- Include more legumes (beans and peas), including baked beans, hummus, lentils, and kidney beans.

- Use natural remedies. Probiotic powders are the first avenue of treatment for all ages. Nutritional supplementation with linseeds (also known as flaxseeds), slippery elm, and psyllium aid in moistening and adding bulk to the stool. For stubborn cases, herbs such as dandelion root, butternut, yellow dock, peppermint, fennel, chamomile, gentian, and liquorice work exceptionally well. Magnesium can be used to help relax and promote muscle movement in the intestine.

- Encourage a regular toileting habit by having your child sit on the toilet for five minutes once or twice a day, preferably after a meal (breakfast is best). Even if they don't do a poo, still encourage this habit. Check out how:

- o Make sure your child is comfortable on the toilet. Provide a stool for him to rest his feet on and make sure his knees are higher than the hips. A toilet seat liner can be handy for little bums. It will help them feel more relaxed because they're not worried about falling into the loo. Any stress may mean your child tightens the pelvic floor muscle, which makes it challenging to have a relaxed toilet session.

- o Encourage your child to lean forward and rest her elbows on her knees.

- o Teach him to push his stomach (abdomen) out when pushing.

- o Make the toilet fun and child friendly with books, toys, or an iPad nearby; the loo can be a tedious and lonely place.

- o "Star" charts are useful to reward your child for sitting on the toilet and doing a poo and can help keep track of progress

- o Encourage exercise and activity. Studies show that sedentary and overweight children get constipation more often.

Sheena's Words of Wisdom: More Poo Help

Kids who are sedentary or overweight are more likely to become constipated, so encouraging more activity and healthful eating are essential for both. Fewer digital toxins and more broccoli, I say.

If your child does get constipated (or has a tummy ache) try massaging her tummy in a *clockwise* direction to encourage muscle contractions moving the food down the digestive tract. Massage up the right side of her stomach, then across the top of the abdomen below the ribcage, then down the left side. I love massaging my children, with or without a health issue as it forms a fabulous connection.

The massage effect will be amplified if you use essential oils. Try a mix of chamomile and lemon balm oils diluted in a carrier oil. It works a treat and smells divine.

Case Study: Poo Problems

Mum brought her nearly five-year-old boy to see me because he had been defecating only every four days for over five months. His doctor had diagnosed him with faecal impaction, in which hard poo packs the intestine and colon tightly, leading to episodes of constipation followed by faecal incontinence that had this poor kid pooing his pants.

The concern was that he was starting school in a few months. Things could be difficult because he often spent a long time in the bathroom. Also, he was fearful that he might mess himself. His mother was concerned that her son was not only in pain, but he would be ridiculed or embarrassed at school.

The doctor had prescribed lactulose, a synthetic sugar used to treat constipation. It often helps to soften the faeces, but the mum did not want the child taking this medicine long term.

The treatment plan:

I agreed with the mother that long-term use of a laxative was not a good idea as often this medicine makes the bowel even more sluggish and lazy, and eventually the bowel forgets how to do the job of contracting and can't push the stools out without assistance. We worked towards reducing medication asap.

We started by treating the cause(s). We improved the diet—increasing fruits, vegetables, and whole foods and cutting down on white and processed foods. The child was also encouraged to drink a full bottle of water every day and fill it up again to ensure adequate fluid.

Then we got the boy out on the trampoline each morning to increase blood flow throughout the digestive system to stimulate digestion and to aid food movement through the gastrointestinal tract.

We encouraged a regular toilet habit as outlined above. And lastly, I got Mum to massage his tummy every night to loosen the stools and stimulate the system.

Over the first month, we reduced the medication and replaced it with an appropriate probiotic powder and an herbal formula containing dandelion root, liquorice and chamomile, which he took two or three times a day. At the end of the month, we reduce the probiotic powder and dose until he didn't need any supplementation at all.

The results:

Within a month, he was passing stools each day unaccompanied, had been weaned off the medication, and was fit and ready to go to school—with the added benefit of an improved diet and more activity. Yay!

Throughout my years of working in health, it is sometimes the simple things that make the difference. We don't need to get too elaborate with our treatments. Back to basics is often the key.

FOOD ALLERGY OR INTOLERANCE. HOW DO YOU KNOW?

One health concern that brings many children to my clinic is a suspected food intolerance or allergy, which isn't surprising given that food allergies have become a major worldwide health concern over the past twenty years. Various statistics indicate that between 6 and 8 per cent of children have a food allergy and that food intolerances are on the rise.

This next section will assist you in working out whether an allergy or intolerance is likely with your child and what to do about it.

Why the increased prevalence of food allergy?

There is a genetic component; kids of parents with allergies at higher risk. However, environmental factors associated with a Western lifestyle seem to be driving this epidemic. Factors may include "the hygiene hypothesis" (see the immunity section), lifestyle changes leading to reduced vitamin D levels, dietary changes, pollutants, and the effect of stress on the immune system.

The introduction of formulas or milk too early may cause problems. The infant's system may be incapable of handling the molecules in the food that are toxic to his body. Cow's milk, which is the most common cause of food allergy in infants and young children, may be a cause of infant colic.

Food allergies in children may be associated with recurring ear infections and inflammation, and with behavioural problems such as attention deficit disorders (ADD and ADHD).

What are food allergies?

We define a food allergy as an exaggerated or abnormal immune system response to a food protein that triggers an allergic reaction: the body treats what should typically be a harmless thing as an alien and mounts an attack on it.

Symptoms tend to be immediate, can be severe, and include hives; itching, watery eyes; swelling of the eyes, lips, throat, and face; vomiting; diarrhoea; nausea; and asthma. In some cases, it can cause potentially life-threatening symptoms, called anaphylaxis, because of either breathing difficulties or a sudden drop in blood pressure. Medicines called antihistamines can relieve most symptoms. Anaphylaxis is treated with epinephrine.

Sometimes food allergy symptoms may be less obvious and can appear as infantile colic, reflux, eczema, diarrhoea, and failure to thrive. Recent studies have found that food allergy may trigger up to 40 to 50 per cent of eczema cases in young children.

Common food allergies

The most common allergies in children are cow's milk and eggs followed by soy, peanuts, tree nuts, and wheat. Some children may react to gluten (causing coeliac disease) or artificial colours and additives.

The good news is that most children lose their allergies by age three to five years. But allergies to peanuts, tree nuts, fish, and shellfish may continue, which is why these four allergies are the most common amongst adolescents and adults.

Sometimes it may be challenging to work out what your child may be allergic to. Allergic disorders include:

Asthma is a respiratory disorder that can cause breathing problems. If the lungs are oversensitive to allergens like dust mites, pollens, or moulds, the bronchioles may become inflamed, swollen, and constricted, which makes it hard to breathe.

Eczema is an itchy rash, also known as atopic dermatitis. Eczema often happens in kids and teens who have allergies, hay fever, or asthma or who have a family history of these conditions.

Allergies of several types can affect children and teens;

- Environmental allergies (for example, dust mites)

- Seasonal allergies (for example, hay fever)

- Drug allergies (for example, specific medications and drugs)

- Food allergies (for example, nuts)

- Allergies to toxins (for example, bee stings)

Why do kids get food allergies?

Genetic predisposition: Often, children will inherit food allergies from their parents. There is a much higher risk of developing allergies if there is a parental history.

Increased gut lining leakiness: The intestinal lining is the barrier that helps to render toxins and baddies harmless. However, gut viral infections and stress may cause inflammation leading to increased permeability or "leakiness" of the lining. Allergens (substances that cause allergies) may then pass through the wall into the bloodstream and cause an allergic reaction.

Maternal consumption and early consumption of allergenic foods: Allergies are less common in infants who are breastfed for three to four months, and there is a lower incidence of allergies in children introduced to common allergenic foods at a later age. To minimize problems, mothers who are breastfeeding and women who are pregnant are advised to avoid foods to which they may have an allergy. Additionally, infants should be breastfed if possible, and the introduction of cow's milk and other highly allergenic foods avoided within the first year of development.

Tip: Cow's milk is often thought to be a woman's primary source of calcium. However, many other sources of calcium do not cause allergic reactions. Good sources include kelp, bok choy, spinach, nuts (examples: almonds and walnuts) and seeds (examples: sesame seeds), tofu, and soy, as well as foods from the cabbage family such as kale and collards.

What are food intolerances?

When conventional tests for allergies show up negative, it is worth considering that an intolerance may be present and not an allergy. With intolerances, a full-blown allergic reaction does not occur, but the child will still experience symptoms brought on by a food. The symptoms may not be obvious but can include, eczema, asthma, digestive upsets, poor sleep habits, or aggressive behaviour. Like allergies, most children grow out of food allergies and intolerances through some sensitivities can last a lifetime.

How are intolerances different from allergies?

Unlike allergies, intolerances *do not* involve the immune system and are more likely to include gut inflammation. A food intolerance is defined as a reproducible toxic response to a food that does not involve the immune system.

The reason children have intolerances is not entirely understood, but several factors seem to play a part, including genetics, the child's gut microbiome (mix of microorganisms in the body and in particular the gut), the frequency of exposure to the particular food, and the immaturity of the gut wall lining.

There are many types of food intolerances. The most common are intolerances to lactose, tyrosine, preservatives, additives, and gluten.

Lactose intolerance is the inability to break down a type of natural sugar called lactose found in dairy products such as milk and yoghurt. A person becomes lactose intolerant when his or her small intestine does not make enough of the enzyme lactase to digest and break down the lactose. When this happens, the undigested lactose moves into the large intestine. The bacteria found in the large intestine interact with the undigested lactose and cause symptoms such as bloating, gas, and diarrhoea.

We can alleviate the symptoms of lactose intolerance by:

- Avoiding milk and milk products

- Drinking lactose-free milk

- Eating more easily digested dairy products such as acidophilus yoghurt, which may not cause symptoms. It contains *Lactobacilli* bacteria, which removes some of the available lactose.

- Taking lactase enzyme in supplement form may help digest lactose.

Tyramine intolerance is the inability to digest the natural food substances tyramine. It can result from eating fermented, aged cheeses and meats, soy products, sauces such as soy and fish, pickled fish, sauerkraut, chocolate, snow peas, edamame beans, avocados, bananas, pineapple, eggplant, figs, red plums, raspberries, peanuts, Brazil nuts, coconut, processed meats, yeast, and beer.

Symptoms of tyramine intolerance can include hives, swelling due to fluid retention, migraines, wheezing, and even asthma. Some researchers suggest that food intolerance or allergy cause as many as 20 per cent of migraines, with tyramine intolerance one of the most common of these toxic responses. In children, cheese and chocolate seem to be the main triggers.

We can alleviate symptoms by:

- Supporting the digestive system (see chapter 2) as well as reducing foods containing pre-formed tyramine.

- Eating foods that help tyramine detoxification—sulphur-containing foods such as onions, Brussels sprouts, garlic, and broccoli.

- Preservatives and additives intolerances can cause adverse reactions, and reports are widely published. Food preservatives include benzoates, sulphites, and hydroxytoluene including butylated hydroxytoluene (BHT), a chemical commonly used in processed foods. Flavouring agents like salicylates and dyes like FD&C Yellow 5 (tartrazine) are known to cause symptoms such as hives.

Carefully reading food labels is one way to avoid some of the food preservatives and additives to which your child may be sensitive; however, when ingredients are present in tiny amounts they are often not declared on the label. I suggest that the best way to avoid potential toxins is to eat fresh, organically grown foods whenever possible.

Gluten intolerance is often discussed separately from food intolerances and food allergies because it has characteristics of both food sensitivities. The sensitivity to gluten is a major component of coeliac disease. However, it seems gluten intolerance without the presence of coeliac is becoming more common. Individuals with this condition have problems with the absorption of nutrients; these problems are made much worse by consuming gluten-containing foods.

Many people get confused, but gluten is not one single substance; rather, it is a mixture of substances. If wheat flour is used to make the dough, and the dough is washed in water until all water-soluble components and starch are rinsed off, the remaining gummy yellowish-grey material consisting of proteins, carbohydrates, fats, and minerals is gluten. About 80 per cent of the gluten material is composed of proteins, and about 20 per cent consists of carbohydrates, fats, and minerals.

Because the gluten in wheat flour creates a beautiful, spongy consistency in bread and other baked items, many manufacturers add it to their baked goods.

Traditionally, wheat, oats, barley, and rye are gluten grains. There are some components of wheat proteins also found in oats and rye, but because it is unclear what portion of the gluten is responsible for allergic reactions, it's hard to understand the role of these other grains in gluten intolerance. Many people who are sensitive to wheat are not equally sensitive to oats, barley, or rye. To be on the safe side, many individuals remove all these foods from their diet when first trying to work out if they are gluten sensitive.

Treating allergies and intolerances

Conventional treatments of food allergies include antihistamines and food avoidance. In most cases, a child will grow out of the allergy, but work with your allergy specialist if you are thinking about introducing an allergenic food back into your child's diet.

Natural treatments offer alternative solutions. Although food intolerances and food allergies cause symptoms in different ways, the use of antiallergenic herbs, where appropriate, for a true food allergy is the only difference in treatment goals. The actions, in summary, may include;

- Identify and remove the offending foods. The only true way to determine the foods that are toxic to your body is to use the elimination diet in which any food that is suspected of causing an allergy or intolerance reaction is removed from the diet and replaced with foods that are least likely to result in a toxic response. Because there is a danger taking food groups out of the diet, an elimination diet must always be carried out under the supervision of a qualified dietitian, nutritionist, or allergy specialist.

- Design a healthy balanced diet to meet the nutritional needs of your child. This may include diets low in histamines, salicylates, amines, gluten, and other food chemicals. The small intestinal bacterial overgrowth (SIBO), low-FODMAP diets, GAPS diet (no grains, pasteurized dairy, starchy vegetables, refined carbs) and other diets may also be used. A word of warning: eliminating food groups for an extended period can be detrimental to your child unless you know what you are doing. Hence, elimination diets must be carried out under the supervision of a qualified health professional.

- Reduce inflammation and improve digestive function, with glutamine, turmeric, gentian, cinnamon, wormwood, slippery elm, liquorice, fish oils, probiotics, zinc, and so forth.

- Use anti-allergic herbs such as albizzia or baical skullcap to dampen an allergic reaction, or the nutraceuticals vitamin C and quercetin.

- Use herbs such as echinacea to normalize the immune response.

- Use gut-healing herbs such as chamomile, marshmallow, calendula, or meadowsweet. Treat symptoms of flatulence or pain with herbs such as peppermint, ginger, lemon balm, or fennel.

The Low-FODMAP Diet

It is worth talking a bit more about this diet as many people with irritable bowel syndrome (IBS) find their symptoms can significantly improve by staying away from foods that contain a family of carbohydrates called FODMAPs (fermentable oligosaccharides, disaccharides, monosaccharides and polyols).

Some dietary ingredients can cause the bowel to stretch and expand because they attract fluid and quickly produce gas when they come in contact with (or are fermented by) bacteria in your bowel. The most common dietary ingredients that do this are the fermentable, poorly absorbed, short-chain carbohydrates. These are sugars that your body can't digest but which become a quick meal for bacteria. These sugars are known as FODMAPs:

Fermentable—rapidly broken down by bacteria in the bowel

Oligosaccharides—fructans and galacto-oligosaccharides (GOS)

Disaccharides—lactose

Monosaccharides—fructose

Polyols—sorbitol, mannitol, xylitol, and maltitol

If this seems too complicated, remember that *saccharide* is a different word for sugar. Polyols are sugar alcohols, or sugar molecules that have an alcohol side chain attached. You might already know some of these sugars or have seen them in ingredients lists on food packaging.

Sheena's Words of Wisdom: Dealing with Allergies and Intolerances

Hopefully by now, you have more of an understanding of how allergies and intolerances differ and whether you suspect your child may have one or the other or both. In most cases, they are not life-threatening. However, I think it is better to be safe than sorry, and if you have any worries at all, get your child along to someone who can help you to sort things out.

I had a client who came to see me about her two young kids. Both the children and the mother were very pale and extremely thin. The children were not thriving, and the woman had gut problems and extreme fatigue. I sent them for blood tests, and the results showed that all three of them had coeliac disease. The mother had been suffering for years without knowing what to do. Years later, all three are flourishing and bouncing with energy. The message here is this: if in doubt, check it out!

The Bottom Line

There is an increased prevalence of food allergy and intolerance. Allergies involve the immune system, whereas intolerances and are more likely to include gut inflammation. Both need a different cause of treatment.

ECZEMA AND OTHER SKIN CONDITIONS

Your skin is the fingerprint of what is going on inside your body, and all skin conditions, from eczema to viral warts and acne, are the manifestations of your body's internal needs.

The skin is one of the most powerful indicators of health. Dry or oily skin, acne, athlete's foot, and inflammatory conditions such as eczema and psoriasis are all signs of poor internal health. However, treating the symptoms only with chemical-laden hydrocortisone creams or medications with heaps of dangerous side effects does little to address the root cause of the problem—poor nutrition and exposure to toxins in the diet and in personal care products, including topical creams, leading to immune system dysfunction and inflammation.

For youngsters, the most common skin condition is eczema. And it can significantly affect your child's schooling and confidence. The itching can drive them up the wall, and some kids feel embarrassed about the red, inflamed, and infected welts. So let's check out what you can do to get your kids skin in tip-top condition—naturally.

Eczema (aka Atopic Dermatitis)

They're red, itchy, and sometimes weepy patches of skin. Scratching worsens them; the patches become scaly, thickened, and infected. They're the calling card of eczema.

Eczema affects about 15–20 per cent of children. Most often, eczema onset occurs before babies are about two years old. In infants, it shows up most often on the cheeks and nappy area. The skin is often dry, scaly, and red with small scratch marks made by sharp baby nails. As the infant becomes a toddler or pre-schooler, eczema commonly affects the outer parts of wrists, elbows, ankles, knees, and genitals. By school age, the same joint creases are affected, and the skin often becomes dry and thickened from constant scratching and rubbing.

Although the medical name for eczema, atopic dermatitis (AD), or allergic skin inflammation, researchers have not yet identified the precise role that allergies play in this condition. They do know that AD seems to run within families with a parent, child or sibling also affected. It also occurs along with other allergic conditions, such as asthma and hay fever.

Research indicates that three types of allergens may contribute to eczema:

Food allergies: These especially include milk, eggs, and peanuts.

Airborne allergens: The most common culprit is the common house dust mite. Others are plant, pollens, animal dander, and mould.

Microbes: Bacteria and yeast can aggravate skin allergies. Many people with eczema also have more bacteria, such as *Staphylococcus aureus* on their skin than do people without the condition. People with eczema are also more likely to develop fungal skin infections and allergic reactions to these fungi.

So what can you do?

Explore and reduce exposure to allergens. Sometimes that can be tricky, but we need to be like a scientist and see if we can pinpoint what is causing the flare-ups.

Food allergies: I get parents to start by removing the common foods that cause food allergies, especially dairy, eggs, and peanuts, but also tomatoes, wheat, sugar, chocolate, yeast extracts, pork, beef, nightshades, and food additives, for at least four days. Watch for changes in the child's skin and overall health. It may help to keep a diet and symptom diary. Then, reintroduce the foods, one at a time, no sooner than every three days. If food recreates or worsens the symptoms, it is at least partly responsible for the condition.

Airborne allergens: These are harder to detect, and this is when a trip to your doctor to get some tests done may be useful. Because the most common culprit is the house dust mite, I often suggest that the house get a good cleaning from top to bottom—particularly the child's bedroom. Bedding should be laundered to get rid of moulds, mites, and pet dander. Change house cleaning materials to ones least likely to cause reactions.

I use essential oils (such as lemon and tea tree) as a base for most of our cleaning needs, and I wash clothes in hypoallergenic detergents. Remember, the reaction may not occur with immediate contact because it can take the immune system a while to identify allergens.

Help for troubled skin

Keep the skin moist. Eczema is a dry-skin condition, so it is necessary to keep the skin moist. Baths hydrate the skin, but use cool water because hot water may aggravate itching. Don't soak too long or bathe too frequently; this will deplete the skin's natural oils. On the few parts of the body that need soap (most do not), use a mild variety. Finally, after the bath, pat excess water rather than rub dry. Immediately apply plenty of body lotion or cream to hold the moisture in. Avoid products with alcohol, synthetic fragrances, or lanolin; use products that incorporate skin-soothing herbs. Your naturopath or medical herbalist can make up a natural vitamin E cream with herbs such as liquorice, St John's wort, chickweed, and chamomile.

Prevent further irritation by avoiding rough-textured clothing, washing clothing with mild soaps and rinsing them thoroughly. Avoid exposure to chemical irritants and any other agents that may cause skin irritation.

Add oats to the bath. Oats have a soothing and moistening effect on the skin. Boil two litres of water, toss in two handfuls of oatmeal, and simmer for ten to fifteen minutes. Strain into a bathtub of water or cool the solution and apply to the skin with a clean cloth. Alternatively, put one to two handfuls of oatmeal into a sock and drop it in the bath as the hot water is running. Use the oat bundle as a sponge on itchy areas. Don't put whole oats directly into the tub—you will end up with a massive cleaning problem, and the resulting "porridge" isn't ideal for the plumbing!

Stop the itch that rashes cause. We need to stop the itch from intensifying. Itching begets scratching, which generates more itching. Ward off scratching before it gets out of hand with a natural anti-itching cream. Finding things to keep your child's hands and brain busy also can help distract from the itch.

Have fun in the sun. Sunlight often clears up eczema. Be sure to reduce the risk of sunburn by keeping exposure to the sun short and wearing a hypoallergenic sunblock. Go indoors if your child starts to feel hot and sweaty, which can aggravate itching.

Boost omega-3 fats. To improve overall health and the health of the skin, eat foods rich in oils: cold-water fish (mackerel, salmon, herring, sardines, anchovies), ground flaxseeds, hempseed, pumpkin seeds, and walnuts, and dark-green leafy vegetables.

Reinoculate the digestive system with good bacteria. In the sections on immunity, digestion, and allergy, we talk about the importance of healthy gut bacteria. We know that eczema and other skin conditions also respond well to inoculation with good bacteria such as *Bifidobacterium lactis*, *Lactobacillus rhamnosus* and *Lactobacillus rheuteri* in the form of a probiotic powder or capsule.

Try herbal medicines and nutraceuticals. Herbal medicines such as echinacea, albizzia, turmeric, baical skullcap, and nettle leaf are used by qualified herbalists to manage skin conditions. Antioxidants such as vitamins A, C, and E; selenium; and zinc are also useful.

Chill out. As I have mentioned before, stress and anxiety play major havoc with our kids' physical, mental, and emotional health. The same goes for the skin. Stressful life events may cause or exacerbate eczema, acne, urticaria, and psoriasis. So, if you think this may ring true of your kid, I suggest reading chapter 6: "A Focus on Your Child's Mental and Emotional Needs."

What about other common skin conditions?

In general, most skin conditions that affect our school-age children include viral warts, herpes simplex virus (HPV) infections. Impetigo (a highly contagious, viral infection of the skin), ringworm or tinea, and acne vulgaris (usually starts in adolescence and adulthood). The scope of this book does not enable me to go into detail treatment options, but in all cases, keeping your child healthy and well through a balanced diet and exercise will go a long way to prevent or minimize the impact of these skin diseases on your child.

Case Study: Itchy Eczema

Baby Jack had been born with perfect skin. Then at the age of three months, after a bout of bronchiolitis, his GP prescribed steroids and antibiotics (after a ten-minute consultation). The parents told me that the doctor thought he might have strep throat. They found out he did not have a bacterial infection, but he had already started the antibiotics and so had to finish the course.

Additionally, the GP suggested they start on solids at four months as Jack was "fussy". Jack was a small baby but well within the recommended percentiles for healthy weight and height.

When Jack was eight months old, his mum and dad brought him to me for a consultation as he had developed atopic eczema inside his elbows and knees and on his cheeks. The eczema was red and inflamed and was causing discomfort as Jack had been scratching the sites on his elbows and behind his knees.

Although Jack had a sunny disposition, he was not sleeping well because of the itching. The GP had prescribed a steroidal cream, but the family were not keen to use it.

The parents had already done an intolerance test which showed wheat and dairy intolerances. The mother had a history of eczema, and the father has coeliac disease.

Treating the cause: It seemed that the antibiotics might have inflamed and injured the gut lining as well as caused a build-up of "bad" microorganisms in the gut. My focus was to reinoculate the intestine with good bacteria, heal the gut, and reduce inflammation.

Because Jack was still being breastfed, we eliminated dairy and wheat from the mother's diet for a trial period of one month while we aimed to repair the baby's gut. We also ensured that Mum was eating a balanced and nutrition-dense diet high in essential fatty acids including fish and flax oils, and probiotic foods, the goodness of which would pass through to Jack via breast milk.

Jack was given a probiotic powder (by popping a small amount onto Mum's nipple when she was breastfeeding), and Mum was provided with my babies' first food diet for Jack to reduce the risk of developing allergies and intolerances. I also recommended the addition of flax oil to Jack's food, such as in his kumara, banana, or avocado puree.

Treating the symptoms: Recognizing how distressing the itching was, I quickly made up a topical cream. The cream contained a base of natural preservative-free vitamin E cream to which I added chickweed and liquorice herbal liquid extracts (alcohol-free), fractionated coconut oil, and melaleuca and lavender essential oils. A day later, the parents emailed to let me know the redness had gone down, and Jack did not seem to be scratching as much.

The results: Jack's eczema quickly healed, and Jack began to sleep much better. Two months later, he has beautiful bright, dermatitis-free skin. It was important to educate the parents about long-term natural health practices to incorporate into their family because of the possible genetic link to allergies and intolerances. In this case, the father had coeliac disease (gluten intolerance) and the mum, a dairy intolerance. The information I provided included advising on optimal diet, nutrition and lifestyle factors to reduce risk or severity of allergies and intolerances, as well as ways to manage the symptoms now and in the future.

WHAT YOU NEED TO KNOW ABOUT URINARY TRACT INFECTIONS AND BEDWETTING

The two most common ailments of the urinary tract that I see in my clinic are urinary tract infections (UTIs) and bedwetting, both of which are incredibly distressing for the child, and in the case of bedwetting, the family.

Urinary tract infections (UTIs)

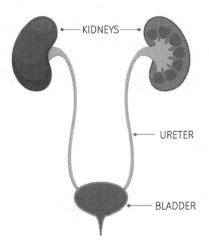

Your urinary tract system

What is the urinary tract, and how does it work?

The urinary tract comprises the kidneys, ureters, bladder, and urethra. The kidneys filter and remove waste and water from the blood to produce urine. The urine travels from the kidneys down two narrow tubes called the ureters to the bladder where it is stored. Then, when your child wees, urine flows through a tube at the bottom of the bladder called the urethra. The opening of the urethra is at the front of the vagina in girls and the end of the penis in boys.

Urinary tract infections (UTIs)

Most UTIs are caused by the bacterium *Escherichia coli* (*E. coli*), which lives in the bowel, the part of the gut where stool changes from liquid to solid. Despite the number of ways the body protects against or fights infections—from a one-way valve where the bladder and ureters attach to urination flushing microbes out of the system—UTIs are still prevalent in kids.

Symptoms of a UTI include:

- Red, pink, cloudy, or foul-smelling urine

- Pain or burning when they urinate (wee)

- Needing to pee often

- Loss of bladder control

- Flank pain, on one or both sides of the back, just below the rib cage and above the waist, or lower belly pain

If the infection is in the bladder or urethra, then it is called cystitis or urethritis respectively, but if they are further up and affect the ureter and kidneys, then it is called pyelonephritis.

How do our kids get UTIs?

- **Bacterial infections.** The most common cause of UTIs is bacteria that usually live in the large intestine and are present in stools, that has travelled through the blood and can cause kidney or bladder infections.

- **Bum wiping skills.** If your child is not wiping his or her bottom well after a bowel motion—back to front and cleaning off all the poo—then the bacteria can get into the urethra and cause an infection.

- **Holding on to urine.** This is common in kids who don't like to pee in toilets they don't know; the practice allows bacteria to grow.

- **Dehydration.** If a child doesn't drink enough fluids, he or she may not make enough urine to flush away bacteria. Busy youngsters often forget to drink.

- **Bunged up.** Constipation can also lead to a UTI because the pebble-like stools may press against the urinary tract, blocking urine flow and providing the perfect environment for bacterial growth.

- **Structural or function problems.** These may reduce the body's ability to eliminate urine. These issues are typically detected at birth or in young infants. They can be serious and may include a structural problem of the bladder that allows urine to flow back to the kidneys (vesicoureteral reflux); kidney stones that block, slow, or disrupt the normal movement of urine; or other abnormalities of the urinary tract.

How can we treat UTIs naturally?

Conventional treatment includes antibiotics, and they certainly are valid, but there are other home treatments you can also try at the first signs of a UTI, which may stop the problem from getting worse and clear up the infection.

- Encourage—but do not force—your child to drink extra fluids as soon as you notice the symptoms and for the next twenty-four hours. More fluid will help make the urine less concentrated and wash out the infection-causing bacteria. Water or cranberry juice is best. Cranberry is well known for its use in the management and prevention of UTIs.

- Encourage your child to urinate often and to empty her bladder each time.

- If there is a fever, refer to chapter 2 for natural fever management tips. A word of warning: cystitis does not typically cause a fever, but infections further up towards the kidneys may do so. Get your child checked out immediately to prevent kidney damage.

- An herbal medicine mix containing herbs such as echinacea, golden rod, corn silk, uva ursi, or liquorice can support symptoms (such as soothing an irritated bladder and reducing pain on urinating) and reduce reinfection by boosting immunity and destroying the baddy bacteria.

Bedwetting

Bedwetting, also known as nocturnal enuresis (NE), refers to unknowingly passing urine while asleep. It is a common problem, and at age five years, 15–25 per cent of children experience NE. So, if your child has this condition, he or she is not alone.

Children do not do this on purpose or out of laziness. It is not a disease but rather a condition that affects the urinary system. It often occurs because of a small bladder, delayed bladder maturation, excessive urine production, urinary tract infection, stress, chronic constipation, or a hormone imbalance.

Some children are deep sleepers, and their brains do not get the signal that their bladders are full. Also, in most cases, bedwetting is an inherited problem, and occurs more often in boys than girls.

Bedwetting is not unusual in kids up to six years of age; however, the impact once your child has started school can be significant. It can seriously affect self-esteem leading to loss of confidence, poor school achievement, and difficulty making friends. Children are often teased and may be reluctant to go on sleepovers or overnight trips. Parent may feel anxious and guilty, may not feel confident in their parenting, and relationships between caregivers and children may suffer.

So what can we do? The good news is that most kids grow out of it, with bedwetting incidence decreasing by 50 per cent each year after age five. You may need to be patient and or use some of the solutions in this section.

Key facts about NE

- Bedwetting occurs slightly more often in boys than girls and is not considered to be a problem until children are about seven years of age.

- NE is common in young children. It affects about 15 per cent of five-year-olds, 5 per cent of ten-year-olds, 2 per cent of fifteen-year-olds, and 1 per cent of adults.

- Almost all children grow out of bedwetting.

- About 1 per cent of adults may still have occasional problems.

Types of bedwetting

There are two types:

- Children who have never been dry for more than a few months at a time have primary enuresis (PNE).

- Children who have been completely dry for more than six months and then start wetting the bed again have secondary enuresis (SNE).

What causes bedwetting?

There is no universal cause, but we know that:

- Bedwetting runs in families.

- The response to wake up if the bladder is full may not have fully developed yet, and so your child does not have conscious control over bedwetting.

- Your child's bladder may not be able to hold the amount of urine that is produced overnight.

- Your child's bladder may be twitchy or overactive; this may cause wet pants or urgency (rushing off to the toilet) in the daytime.

- There is often an association between SNE, anxiety, and social withdrawal, which may lead to reduced appetite and constipation, contributing to enuresis.

- Bedwetting is rarely due to urine infection, disease, or child abuse

- Some children bed wet because of sleep disorders, including obstructive sleep apnea. If your child snores, this might be a sign that the bedwetting is an unexpected sign of sleep apnea.

Treating bedwetting

Allopathic treatment: The most common treatment is the bedwetting alarm, which has been reported to have up to a 70 per cent success rate. The alarm awakens your sleeping child as soon as he or she wets the bed and eventually trains the child to wake up before urination occurs. Alarms are more likely to work if your child is keen and if you have professional support. Although I recognize they have a use, I feel it is quite mean to wake your child in the middle of the night; this can be traumatic and exhausting for the child.

Lab tests on blood and urine may be performed to rule out a medical condition if there is daytime wetting or bedwetting starts up after more than a year of dry beds. Scans or x-rays are not usually needed.

Conventional treatment may also include drug prescriptions. These should be avoided at all costs because of potential safety concerns and adverse outcomes.

Natural treatment includes:

- Regulating fluid intake. Encourage your child to drink good quantities of fluid but try to limit intake after 6 pm so that he doesn't go to bed with a full bladder. Avoid any caffeine-containing drinks such as tea, chocolate, or fizzy drinks. They act as diuretics.

- Bladder training. Bedwetting accidents at night may be relieved by learning bladder training exercises that strengthen muscles and increase bladder capacity. The initial step is to focus on the amount of time that your child can retain the urine when the sense to pee first happens. This effort helps to strengthen the muscles needed to prevent accidents.

- Therapies such as motivational therapy, hypnotherapy and acupuncture may be useful in conjunction with bladder training or the use of medication.

- Herbal medicines and supplements to assist with stress and anxiety, bladder tone, infections, constipation and inflammation. These may include, chamomile, St John's wort, cramp bark, crataeva, echinacea, liquorice, goldenrod, and marshmallow root. A qualified naturopath and herbalist will make up a prescription specific to your child's needs.

What can you do?

- Work with your health professional to discover and treat the cause.

- Ensure the child has a healthy appetite and regular bowel motions.

- Children need routines and to know they are loved and respected. They need adequate sleep, a healthy diet, and fun and play.

- Allow your child to be involved and have a say in the treatment plan.

- Be patient and understanding; reassure your child, especially if he is upset.

- Praise and reward your child for getting up to use the toilet and having a dry night.

- Respond gently when your child wets the bed even if you feel angry.

- Prepare the bed and your child. Use a thick plastic mattress cover and protect the mattress with absorbent pads or towels. It might help to stop your child from flooding the bed if she wears extra-thick underwear and pyjamas.

- Give your child plenty of fluid during the day to help the bladder to get used to holding larger amounts of urine.

- Avoid any caffeine-containing drinks such as tea, chocolate, or fizzy drinks. They act as diuretics.

- Get your child to wee before bedtime.

- If you wake your kid up to wee after he has been asleep for several hours, it is vital to make sure he is fully awake. Be mindful that waking him up during the night to go to the toilet might help, but he could end up missing too much sleep.

- Shower or bathe your child in the morning before school; otherwise, the smell of urine might be embarrassing and lead to teasing.

- If a child is having a sleepover, discretely discuss the situation with the host parent and hide a pull-up nappy in the bag for your child to use.

- Teach your child anxiety and stress-reducing techniques such as mindfulness and breathing exercises (see chapter 6).

- Consider counselling to allow the child—and the rest of the family—to talk through the issues.

What are some things you shouldn't do?

- Don't punish your child for what he can't control

- Don't use nappies or plastic pants if the child is over four years old and is embarrassed.

When should I get some professional help?

Make an appointment with your health care provider who may be able to assist or put you in touch with a specialist in this area of health. Get help in these circumstances:

- The child is wetting during the day

- The child has suddenly started to wet the bed again after over a year of being dry

- The child is still bedwetting after age six or seven, and it is upsetting her

- The bedwetting is causing problems in the family

STRESS, ANXIETY, AND BEHAVIOUR

This is such a large topic that I have written a whole chapter on mental health. Check out chapter 6: "A Focus on Your Child's Mental and Emotional Needs" for more on stress and anxiety.

Chapter 3

MORE PEAS, PLEASE— KIDS' EATING HABITS AND DIET

Now we have food. I can concentrate better in
class. I used to want just to sleep.
                                    —*Seven-year-old Josh*

When it comes to a child's health, I always go back to three essential things;

1. Is your child loved? No? Then love her.

2. Is your child nourished? No? Then nourish him.

3. Is your child being coached? No? Then coach her.

Honestly, it's as simple as that. No amount of extra-curricular activities, pocket money, treats or private tutoring is as important as the time spent with your child, cuddling, laughing or showing him the way forward, what is right or wrong, or providing the most nutritious food and drink possible.

WHAT SHOULD YOUR CHILD BE EATING?

What your child puts into her body is at the root of your child's short- and long-term mental and physical health and happiness. That is why I have devoted a large chunk of this book to the what, why, and how of providing your child with a nourishing diet.

In the thirty years I have worked in the field of nutrition and health, I have experienced many food and nutrition trends, fads, and theories. Today it seems to me that people are more confused than ever before about what they should be consuming.

More and more often families, or individuals in families, are following an eating plan that is gluten or dairy free, avoids sugar, is paleo driven, low in carbohydrates, high in fat, yeast-free, or raw. You name it; I've heard it. A question I now ask most of my patients is, "What rules do you have in your family about food?"

What gets me, though, is that, despite this increased interest in diet, we see that obesity, fatty liver disease, diabetes, and allergies and intolerances are all on the rise. So are these strict diets, which often omit a whole food groups, really that good? I say, no!

Okay, some of you are going to want to close the book now, but please hear me out before you do. I reckon that we will be healthier and happier if we spend less time and money following unfounded weird diets, often designed by people with little nutrition experience, or buying so-called superfoods. Instead, let's focus on:

- Teaching our kids how to cook

- Cooking from scratch, rather than throwing down processed, ready-in-a-minute meals

- Spending more time eating together as a family

- Tending a vegetable garden—communal or in your backyard

- Playing outside—both kids and adults and ditching digital toxins

- Spending less time on "succeeding" and more time being with our kids

It seems to me that getting back to basics, as many of our parents and grandparents used to eat and live, has its merits.

The Greek physician Herophilus (335–280 BC) said: "When health is absent, wisdom cannot reveal itself, art cannot manifest, strength cannot fight, wealth becomes useless, and intelligence cannot be applied."

I know that you, like me, wish to support your kids and help them reach their full potential and lead amazing lives. For this to happen, they must be healthy.

During my long career as a nutritionist and a naturopath, and through reading, research, and clinical practice, I have come to recognize that malnourishment is the cause of many illnesses. Let's say a person has aching joints or arthritis. A medical doctor might treat this with anti-inflammatories, whereas I want to find out whether the patient is producing enough digestive juices. If he is not, is food getting broken down? Has the situation led to nutrient malabsorption? Then, if the partially digested food had crossed the gut into the blood, had this started an inflammatory reaction, in this case, in the joints?

So, my philosophy is to start by looking for the nutrient or nutrients that may be lacking and rebalancing these rather than treating only the symptoms.

As you will be starting to understand, we can prevent and treat many illnesses and imbalances naturally without pharmaceutical medication. The place to start is by ensuring the best possible diet for your loved ones. If your child has recently started school, then proper nutrition is going to be paramount, and it may pay to consider the role of food in brain performance and focus, stress and anxiety management, immunity and sustained energy. Kids will be stretching their mental and physical capacity learning new things, adapting to a new environment, warding off bugs, and spending long days at school.

So let's spend the next few pages learning the art of healthful eating. How can we can use the power of food as our children's primary medicine?

Nutrition basics

I believe that many of the parents who consult me are so overwhelmed by the amount of conflicting nutrition knowledge out there that they are not sure what to think or put on the table. All I can do is give you some nutrition basics, which, through years of tradition and often backed up with evidence-based research, have kept our ancestors living long and quality lives.

Before we start, just a reminder that childhood is a time for rapid growth and development. Because of this, the nutritional needs of children differ from those of adults. For example, kids require more carbohydrates but less fibre (depending on ages and activity levels) than adults. Often, I find adults are imposing their dietary rules on their children (with the best intentions, of course); but they can be doing more harm than good.

To be able to understand what to eat, it may help to be reminded of or learn the fundamentals of nutrition.

Food is made up of nutrients

Food provides a range of different nutrients. Some nutrients provide energy while others are essential for growth and maintenance of the body. Carbohydrates, protein, and fat are macronutrients that we need to eat in relatively significant amounts because they provide our bodies with energy and the building blocks for the growth and maintenance of a healthy body. Vitamins and minerals are micronutrients, which are needed only in small amounts but are essential for keeping us healthy. Some food components that are not strictly nutrients are necessary for health, such as water and fibre.

Macronutrients

Carbohydrates: The body's primary fuel source	Carbohydrates are vital, providing energy for the body and brain because every cell in the body, including the brain, requires a constant supply of glucose as fuel, and glucose is a building block of carbohydrates in food and drink.
Sources: **Complex carbohydrates:** Wholemeal bread, wholemeal pasta, brown rice, oats, all fruits and vegetables **Refined carbohydrates:** Sugar, chocolate, chippies, cakes, biscuits, and soft drinks.	Carbohydrates are necessary for growing children because they have a greater need for energy than adults. We group carbohydrates as complex, or refined or straightforward; **Complex carbohydrates** include whole grain bread, wholemeal pasta, brown rice, muesli, legumes, beans and peas, nuts and seeds. Complex carbohydrates can lower blood cholesterol, regulate blood sugar levels and bowel movements, reduce the appetite, and maintain energy levels. **Refined carbohydrates** include sugar, chocolate, chippies, cakes, biscuits and soft drinks. These should be limited in a healthy diet because they also tend to be full of "bad" fats and added sugars. Eating too many of these can lead to diabetes and obesity. **Fibre** is an indigestible form of carbohydrate. Fruits, vegetables, and whole-grain foods all contain high amounts of fibre. Since humans cannot break down roughage, fibre pass through the digestive system whole and takes other waste products with them. Diets low in fibre have problems with waste elimination, constipation, and haemorrhoids. Diets high in fibre have shown decreased risk for obesity, high cholesterol, and heart disease.

	Carbohydrates and glycaemic index (GI)
	Carbs are vital, providing energy for the body and brain. The glycaemic index tells us how quickly the body digests a particular carbohydrate. In high-GI foods, such as lollies, the starch is broken down and absorbed into the blood quickly, causing blood glucose (sugar) levels to rise.
Protein: Necessary for growth, repair, and development **Sources:** Chicken, fish, beef, pork, eggs, milk, cheese yoghurt, nuts, seeds, pulses, lentils, quinoa, soy products, yoghurt, tofu	**Protein** is essential for growth, repair, and development. It provides the body with sustainable energy that is needed for the manufacture of hormones, antibodies, and enzymes. It is vital in building healthy skin, hair, nails, cartilage, bones, and ligaments. It also helps maintain the proper acid-alkali balance in the body. Protein is made up of twenty amino acids; nine of these are essential and, because the body can't make them, must be gained through diet. Proteins that contain all nine essential amino acids are "high-quality" proteins. All animal foods, soy protein and quinoa are high-quality proteins. Proteins that don't contain all nine essential amino acids are considered "low-quality" proteins; most come from plant sources. **Animal sources:** meat, eggs, fish, milk, cheese and yoghurt. Animal protein is also an excellent source of easily absorbable iron and Vitamin B12. **Plant sources:** grains (quinoa, oats, barley), nuts, seeds, and pulses (dried beans, some types of peas and lentils), soy.

Fats: The right fats are essential for healthy development and functioning of the brain, nervous system, eyes, skin, and hormonal balance.

Foods that contain fats also provide us with the fat-soluble vitamins A, D, E, and K.

Keep sugary treats to a minimum as the body stores excess carbohydrates as fat.

There are two types of fats—**saturated,** which mostly comes from animal sources, and **unsaturated** which comes from vegetable foods.

Saturated fats are found in animal products (meat and dairy foods) and some plant oils (coconut and palm oils). These fats are a source of energy and are part of our cell membranes. Too much saturated fat may play a role in cardiovascular disease and an increased risk of some cancers. These are the "bad" fats; however, it is important to have some of these fats in your diet as they contain the fat-soluble vitamins A, D, E and K—but don't include too much of them! Eating too much saturated fat may raise blood cholesterol levels and increase the chance of getting heart disease.

Unsaturated fats are an essential part of the diet found in foods such as vegetable oils (cold-pressed are best), nuts, seeds, fish, avocadoes, and some vegetables.

What are essential fatty acids?

Omega-3 and omega-6 are types of unsaturated fats known as essential fatty acids (EFAs) because they can't be made by the body and must be eaten. Essential fatty acids are necessary for the function of most tissues in the body. Deficiencies can lead to scaly and dry skin, infertility, and impaired immune function. In general, our Western diets contain too many omega-6 fatty acids and too few omega-3 fatty acids. To equal the balance, eat fewer processed foods and processed vegetable oils (sunflower, corn, and soybean) and more olive and avocado oil, oily fish, nuts, and seeds.

A word about coconut oil.

Coconut oil is touted as a superfood. I say there are no superfoods but only super diets. I am also concerned because many of my patients tell me they have moved from other oils to solely using coconut oil, which is not the best idea, as you will find out as you read on. By all means, incorporate a small amount into your diet if you wish, but also consume a variety of other oils including fish, flax, olive, and avocado—and a small amount of butter.

The low down: Coconut oil has some antioxidant properties because of plant nutrients called phenolic compounds. It's an unusual blend of short- and medium-chain fatty acids not seen in other saturated fats, which may provide health benefits. However, research is yet to confirm this. Coconut oil can be *part* of a healthy diet, but it is not super special. Plant oils provide health benefits, particularly extra virgin olive oil, which has proven health benefits.

The thing we shouldn't ignore is that coconut oil is high in saturated fat (more than in butter) so it is considered a solid fat. One of the main concerns is the fatty acids found in the fat found in coconut oil raise LDL (the bad cholesterol) just like other saturated fats such as butter. We know that our diets have too much saturated fat already. And while coconut may also raise HDL cholesterol (the good cholesterol), it doesn't do this as much as unsaturated fats do. Okay, coconut oil doesn't contain cholesterol, but it still doesn't stack up against most other plant-based oils such as canola, corn, safflower, sunflower, soybean, flaxseed, grapeseed, and extra virgin olive oil, which all contain much less saturated fat. Lastly, have you seen the price!

Handy hint: Going out for a long bike ride or walk? Remember to take some complex carbohydrates with you to keep your energy up. Bananas, nuts, and low-sugar muesli bars are ideal. Take some water too! Kids need several servings of natural carbohydrates a day such as whole-grain cereal and bread, pasta, pulses, and potatoes to stay on top both physically and mentally. Because children are often more active than adults, they need to eat more carbs.

Handy hint: The skins of fruits and vegetables are a good source of fibre, so it is better to wash rather than peel them. Be careful you don't overdo the fibre for kids as this can stop the absorption of many vitamins and minerals.

The micronutrients—vitamins and minerals

Sufficient quantities of fresh, quality food will provide most children with all the vitamins and minerals they need. The children most at risk of deficiencies are vegan kids. Parents must make sure their diet contain adequate nutrients—protein, iron, zinc, omega 3, and vitamin B12, in particular. Children who are picky eaters may also be at risk and may benefit by taking a high-quality children's multivitamin and mineral supplement.

Vitamins: There are two types of vitamins—fat-soluble (vitamins A, D, E, and K) and water-soluble (B-complex and vitamin C). The body can store fat-soluble vitamins, and so we do not need to consume them every day. We can't store water-soluble vitamins, though, so we need to eat foods containing these daily. Water-soluble vitamins are destroyed by overcooking. The best way to serve fruits and vegetables is to steam them, quickly stir-fry them, or eat them raw.

Minerals: We all need minerals in small quantities; they have many functions in the body including growth and immune function and regulating body fluids and bone mass.

Nutrient	Function	Good food sources
Vitamins		
Vitamin A	Necessary for growth, healthy skin, tooth enamel, and good vision.	Liver, oily fish, carrots, dark green vegetables, kumara (sweet potato), oranges, pumpkin, tomatoes, lentils, apricots, peaches, whole milk, eggs.
Vitamin B Complex B1 (Thiamine) B2 (Riboflavin) B3 (Niacin) B6 (Pyridoxine) B12 (Cobalamin) Folic acid (Folate)	Essential for growth, energy production, healthy blood and nervous system, digestion. B vitamins impact every cell in the body. B vitamins have an important role in converting carbohydrates, protein, and fat to energy. Each B vitamin has a specific role to play. For example, vitamin B12 is essential for healthy blood and nerves. Folate and vitamin B12 aid energy and genetic material.	Thiamine: whole grains, nuts, meat, breakfast cereals. Riboflavin: milk, eggs, liver, green vegetables, breakfast cereals. Niacin: Meat, breakfast cereals. B6: Beef, fish, and poultry, eggs, whole grains, some vegetables. B12: meat, milk and eggs and yeast extracts. Folate: dark leafy green vegetables (kale, silverbeet, spinach, kale), liver, bananas, avocados, oranges, bread peanuts, legumes (dried beans and peas), breakfast cereals.

Vitamin C	Necessary for growth, wound healing, immune function, and iron absorption.	Most vegetables and fruits.
Vitamin D	Essential for bone formation as it works with calcium.	Oily fish, liver, eggs, dairy. Produce
Vitamin E	A component of all body cells; it and helps the body to create red blood cells.	Vegetable oils, wheat germ, nuts.
Vitamin K	Necessary for blood clotting and intestinal health.	Most vegetables and wholegrain cereals.

Minerals		
Calcium	Needed for strong bones, good teeth, and growth.	Dairy products (milk, cheese, yoghurt); fortified nut, oat or rice milk; canned fish with bones (like sardines); tofu; some nuts (such as almonds); sesame seeds; broccoli; pulses; and fortified breakfast cereals.
Iron	Necessary for healthy blood and muscles. Iron is one of the most common deficiencies among children and will leave them feeling tired and run down.	Red meat, oily fish, egg yolks, dried fruits, wholegrain cereals, legumes, green leafy vegetables.

Iodine	Essential for optimum thyroid gland function. The thyroid is responsible for our metabolic rate (how quickly we burn energy) as well as growth and brain development; it needs iodine to work. Iodine deficiency can affect mental performance and hearing.	Seaweed, seafood and fish, dairy and eggs. Bread in New Zealand is now fortified with iodine (except for organic and salt-free bread, and some bread mixes). *Note: New Zealand soils are low in iodine, resulting in low iodine levels in locally grown foods.*
Magnesium	Magnesium plays a vital role in over 300 biochemical reactions in the body: nerve, muscle, and heart function; keeping bones strong; producing energy; and immune function.	Excellent sources include dark green, leafy vegetables, other vegetables or fruit (bananas and avocados), nuts (cashews and almonds), peas and beans, seeds, soy products, whole grains, milk.
Selenium	Selenium is an antioxidant that protects our body against damage. Selenium helps to keep our immune system healthy as well as regulate blood pressure and balance mood.	Rich sources include Brazil nuts, eggs, fish, brown rice, chia seeds and other seeds, meat, shitake mushrooms, green leafy vegetables.

Sodium	A small amount of sodium is needed to keep our body fluids and electrolytes balanced. We may need to replace sodium lost through excessive sweating during exercise or manual labour. Too much salt in our diet may lead to raised blood pressure, which is a risk factor for heart disease, stroke, and kidney disease.	Choose low-salt foods containing less than 120 milligrams salt per 100 grams of food. In modern diets, only 10 per cent of salt consumed occurs naturally in food; 15 per cent is added while cooking or at the table. The rest comes from processed and manufactured food. Eat fresh is best!
Zinc	Zinc is needed for the body's immune (defence system) to work. It plays a role in cell and skin health, growth, wound healing, smell, and taste.	Beef, pork, lamb (meat contains more zinc than fish), nuts, whole grains, legumes, and yeast

DIGESTION 101

Understanding what happens to our food once it has entered the mouth and the waste has come out the other end is not only super fascinating (for me anyway), but it can also help you to understand the importance of great nutrition and eating habits. So here goes—a quick reminder of how our digestive system works.

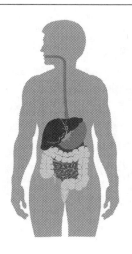

MOUTH

Digestion starts when we chew or smell food, releasing saliva to begin the breakdown of carbohydrates

OESOPHAGUS

Muscles contract and relax to push the food into your stomach

STOMACH

Everything blends. Hydrochloric acid kills bugs and along with enzymes break down proteins

LIVER

Fats are broken down by bile stored in the liver

PANCREAS

Many digestive enzymes are stored here and used to break down our food

SMALL INTESTINE

Where 80% of the nutrients and minerals from food are absorbed into the bloodstream

LARGE INTESTINE

Absorbs water from the remaining indigestible food matter and transmit the waste from the body

ANUS

Solid waste leaves your body

Your digestive system

NUTRITION TIPS TO KEEP YOUR KIDS FIGHTING FIT

Our role as parents and caregivers is to provide our children with healthy, nutritious meals. Their role is to eat it.

Is your child happy most of the time, energetic, thriving physically and emotionally and gaining weight and height, active and interested, and communicating well? Yes? Then relax—you are doing a great job giving your kid what she or he needs.

If this is not the case, and you could do with a few tips about "grub for your cub", then read on. These ten tips are a good starter for ensuring your kids are in top condition.

Tip one: Seasonal and fresh foods are best

Fresh food is usually of better quality than processed foods (frozen, canned, or packaged foods) and contains fewer preservatives. Often they are higher in nutrient levels, and nine times out of ten, they taste better.

Seasonal fresh foods are even better because not only are they cheaper, but they haven't lost any nutrients in storage. Fruits and veggies possess properties in the same way that medicinal herbs do, so eating foods in season means you are automatically eating the foods you need at that time of year. For example, foods are often lighter and juicier in summer—think strawberries, oranges, and lettuce. They provide fluid to prevent dehydration in the sun, and they are easier to digest. Winter foods tend to be denser. Imagine casseroles and soups, which produce more fuel to heat the body. In general, summer foods are cooling and should include juicy fruits and salad-style vegetables. Winter foods are warming and should include beans, legumes, and root vegetables.

What's the deal with processed foods? Are they that bad?

When I am talking about processed foods, I mean those that have been chemically treated and made solely from refined ingredients and artificial substances. There are various degrees of processing. For example, I am not opposed to using tinned vegetables, fruit (no sugar), or whole beans or whole frozen foods because they are not chemically changed, and they retain most of their nutrients. However, I would discourage everyday consumption of processed foods containing:

Preservatives: Chemicals that prevent the food from rotting.

Colourants: Chemicals that are used to give the food colour.

Flavour: Chemicals that give the food a taste.

Texturants: Chemicals that give texture.

Processed foods tend to be high in refined, "simple" carbohydrates. These lead to rapid spikes in blood sugar and insulin levels and may cause adverse health effects such as obesity and diabetes. They also tend to be high in cheap and refined unhealthy oils and low in nutrients and fibre. Fresh food does taste better too.

Whole foods require more energy to digest than processed foods. A study compared two sandwiches that had the same number of calories and macronutrients; one sandwich was made with a grainy bread and cheddar cheese, while the other made with white bread and processed cheese slices. The interesting thing is those who ate the whole grain sandwich burned twice as many calories while eating the meal.

We require a balance of healthy macronutrients (protein, fat, and carbohydrates), micronutrients (vitamins, minerals, antioxidants, phytochemicals), and adequate phytonutrients, enzymes, fibre, and water to function.

If we replace whole foods with foods selected because they are convenient—low-calorie, low-carb, high-protein, or low-fat, for example—we start missing essential nutrients. For example, low carbs may lead to low energy, low fat to poor brain function or hormone imbalance, high protein to kidney overload. Before we know it, the body becomes malnourished and is not performing as it should.

A varied, whole-foods diet will also naturally offer a relatively low glycaemic index (GI). As I discussed earlier, the carbs in a low-GI food slowly break down to sugar in the bloodstream, promoting sustained energy and fewer hunger pangs. And, they reduce the risk of obesity and diabetes. Foods with a low GI and high nutrient composition include fruits, veggies, nuts, beans, seeds, and whole grains.

Tip two: Variety is the spice of life

It's crucial to eat varied and exciting foods every day including food from all the core food groups: vegetables and fruit; bread and cereals; milk, yoghurt, and cheese; and meat and alternatives (such as beans and tofu). Variety provides all the nutrients—vitamins and minerals, phytonutrients, protein, carbohydrates and fats—to keep you healthy. It also makes eating exciting, so you enjoy what you eat.

No child is going to enjoy food if the same old thing is put in front of him or her every day. Variety also means a variety of textures—crunchy vegetables, grains to chew on, custards, stewed fruits. It means colour—aim for orange, red, purple, and green fruits and vegetables. Try different meal ideas and a variety of foods each day to keep them interested in healthy eating and to maintain or achieve health and vitality today and long after they have left the nest.

> **Handy Hint:** Healthy food does not have to taste bland and boring, and there's no need to eat foods that are unpalatable just because "they're good for you". Invest in a good cookbook or search online for easy nourishing meals to give you some ideas for food preparation and recipes. Have fun experimenting!

Tip three: Keep hydrated

As most of our body is made up of water, we must drink a lot to replace fluids and to ensure we remain hydrated. If we drink enough water, it means our body can work to maximum efficiency. As a rough measure, adults need to drink about two litres, and kids one litre a day. Keep hydrated if the weather is scorching or if you have engaged in lots of activity. As a rule of thumb, you are already dehydrated if you feel thirsty.

Handy Hint: Steer clear of sugar-laden fizzy drinks. Plain water is best; you can try tap water or mineral water, plain or flavoured, sparkling or non-sparkling. Milk, diluted fruit juices, soft drinks, and tea are okay occasionally. Each child should a personal drink bottle to prevent germs from spreading.

Whats on your kids plate?

Tip four: How much is on the plate?

We often pile too much food on our kids' (and our own!) plates. Try serving food on a small dish, such as a side plate, so that the amount on the plate seems much larger. A kid's plate should contain one-third veggies, fruit, or salad; one-third protein; and one-third carbohydrates. Growing and active kids should have more carbs and a little less protein. I use the plate model all the time because it is easy for wee ones and adults to remember. Soon your family will be regularly tucking into balanced, delicious, and varied meals

Tip five: Stock up with the right ingredients

The first step in creating balanced meals is to have the right ingredients in your fridge, freezer, and pantry. Check out Appendix One for a shopping list to help you to stock up with some nutritious food items. A fantastic way to get kids eating more of the right stuff is to take them food shopping. Start with a list and let them know that you are purchasing only what is on the list—this should stop them asking for the not-so-healthy.

When you're at the supermarket, let children run off to find shopping items for you. Ask their advice on which foods to buy—berries or peaches, spaghetti ribbons or twirls. Check out the nutritional information with your kids. As a starter, show them how to find out how much sugar is in their favourite muesli bars, cereals, and drinks.

Tip six: Eat your fruit and veggies

Fruits and vegetables are great sources of nutrients—vitamins, minerals, phytonutrients, trace elements, essential fatty acids, antioxidants, and fibre—that help us keep healthy. Five or more servings a day is a good amount. If your kids are eating two portions of fruit and three portions of vegetables a day (a portion is about the size of the palm of your hand), then you are doing well. The more, the better.

> **Handy Hint:** So that you don't lose too many nutrients, the best way to cook veggies is to steam, stir-fry, roast, or bake them (no need to microwave or boil them to death!), or of course eat them raw. Fruit is best eaten whole (rather than juiced) to retain the fibre and to slow down the absorption of sugars.

Tip seven: Snack attack

Even if your kids eat regular meals during the day, there will still be times in between when they feel hungry, especially if they are physically active. Snacks can fill the gap but should be eaten as extras and not in place of meals. There are lots of different snacks available. I suggest yoghurt (unsweetened, probiotic), a handful of fresh or dried fruits, sticks of vegetables like carrots and celery with hummus or nut butter, Edam or cottage cheese, unsalted nuts, oat or rice crackers, or perhaps a slice of fruit loaf or some grainy bread with avocado and feta. Occasionally it's okay to have treat foods such as a packet of chips, cake, biscuits, or chocolate as snacks—say once a week.

Tip eight: Food is fun

Sharing a meal with family and friends at home or school is a great way to enjoy food. It is fun to see and discuss other people's choice of food. What do your friends eat? Do you try different foods every day? Check out your lunch box or dinner plate. How many kinds of fruits and vegetables can you spot?

Tip nine: Make it taste good

You will be surprised how kids take to herbs and spices as flavourings. Try mild chilli or curry powders, garlic, turmeric, paprika, cinnamon, basil, parsley, coriander. There are many to try in your cooking instead of butter, tomato sauce, and other processed sauces. Do not salt their food—use lemon, herb, or kelp salt instead.

Tip ten: Reduce or restrict sugar

Okay, we've now let the dinosaur out of the bag—sugar! We know it's not good for us, we are aware there are links between high sugar intake and tooth decay, obesity, diabetes, and other diseases, and we know that many of us need to reduce how much sugar we consume. So let's take a look at sugar and get more of an understanding of how much is too much.

How much sugar should we eat? In 2015 The World Health Organisation (WHO) put out a new guideline that recommends adults and children reduce their daily intake of free sugars to less than 10 per cent of their total energy intake. A further reduction to below 5 per cent or roughly 25 grams (6 teaspoons) per day would provide additional health benefits.

Total, free sugars and added sugars—what's the difference? *Total* sugars refer to the full amount of sugars in food, including the sugars found naturally in fruit, vegetables, and milk. *Free* sugars are monosaccharides (such as glucose and fructose) and disaccharides (such as sucrose or table sugar) added to foods and drinks by manufacturers, cooks, or consumers, and sugars naturally present in honey, syrups, fruit juices, and fruit juice concentrates. Added sugars include all monosaccharides and disaccharides added to food by manufacturers, cooks, and consumers.

Natural or intrinsic sugars are those sugars naturally occurring and not added. These sugars are an integral part of the food such as fructose in fruit and lactose in milk.

So what should we do to reduce sugar? The WHO guideline does not refer to the sugars in fresh fruits and vegetables and sugars naturally present in milk because there is no reported evidence of adverse effects of consuming these sugars.

Parents come to a consultation about their child's health issues with me and swear blind that their kids aren't eating much sugar and that they don't guzzle down fizzy drinks or plates of biscuits. And I believe them. However, much of the sugars consumed today are "hidden" in processed foods. For example, one tablespoon of ketchup contains around 4 grams (around one teaspoon) of free sugars. A single can of sugar-sweetened soda contains up to 40 grams (about ten teaspoons) of free sugars. You can see how sugar can add up quite quickly without you even knowing it.

The scary thing is sugar added to many foods, like bread, condiments, and sauces, don't even taste all that sweet. So, unless we start reading the labels, we aren't aware of heaps of sugar we are giving our kids.

CUTTING BACK ON YOUR KIDS' SWEET TREATS

Limit foods and beverages with added sugars. The first step is to reduce your kid's exposure to sugary drinks and foods. I go by the 80/20 rule. If your child eats a few lollies at a party or a family occasion, then that is fine if the rest of the time sugar intake is low. Foods that have a load of added sugar include fizzy drinks, sports and energy drinks, juice, syrup, muffins, cakes and biscuits, ice cream and sorbet, and other desserts. But they can also be found in sauces such as ketchup and tinned baked beans.

Serve small portions. Have the occasional lollies, chocolate, or dessert, but in small amounts. I suggest small bowls and side plates, small-portion-size chocolate bars or lolly packs, or sharing a super-sized cupcake or muffin.

Avoid the supermarket check-out line that has the sweet treat display. Waiting in a check-out aisle in front of a smorgasbord of goodies is a sure-fire way to get kids wanting treats. Aim for the lolly-free aisle, *and* make sure you have fed the children before shopping so they are not as likely to need food while you are out.

Focus on using non-food items as a reward. If we offer our kids food as a reward for achieving a goal or for good behaviour, they learn to think that some foods are better than other foods. Reward your child with big hugs, love, words, or non-food items like stickers or balloons to make them feel acknowledged as the extraordinary wee persons they are.

Ditch the fizzy. "Soft drink" refers to beverages with added sugar or another sweetener, and include soda, fruit punch, lemonade, sweetened powdered drinks, and sports and energy drinks. *One can of sugary drink a day can lead to 6.5 kilograms of weight gain in a year.*

Dish up fruit or vegetable as dessert. Ditch the calorie-laden puddings and ice cream and instead serve baked apples or pears stuffed with nuts, a seasonal fruit salad, an avocado mousse, carrot and coconut pudding, or frozen fruit ice blocks. Better still, make dessert an occasional, not a daily, occurrence.

Make food fun. Let's make nutritious foods just as enticing as those that are sugar laden. Be creative and whacky with your child and make fruity, veggie pictures or faces with sliced bananas, carrot sticks, raisins, and grapes, and then gobble them all up.

Be a food scientist. Let children loose in the kitchen to make new healthy snacks. Provide the ingredients—from nut butters and wholegrain cereals to dried fruit and cheese—and then allow your children go wild inventing new foods.

Play sugar detectives in the supermarket. Show kids how to find the total sugars in various cereals, drinks, and muesli bars. Then set them the challenge of finding the cereals, bars and drinks with the highest and lowest sugar. Don't forget to help them understand how their favourites rank.

Make treats "treats" rather than everyday foods. Occasional treats are fine; just don't make them an everyday thing. If kids don't eat their meals, they don't need sweet "extras".

KID MEAL PLANNING GUIDELINES: HOW MUCH DO WE NEED TO EAT?

Earlier in the chapter, I talk about using the plate model: a plate should contain one-third veggies, fruit, or salad; one-third protein; and one-third carbohydrates. Growing and active kids should have more carbs and a little less protein. However, the guidelines developed by the New Zealand Ministry of Health may also help you to make sure your kids are getting the best nutrition for their age:

Suggested daily requirements

1. **Vegetables and fruit: These contain carbohydrates, fibre, vitamins, and minerals.**

    For preschoolers: at least two servings of vegetables and two servings of fruit each day.

    School children: at least three servings of vegetables and two servings of fruit each day.

    Vegetable serving examples: one medium potato or root vegetable (135 grams); 1/2 cup cooked vegetables; 1/2 cup salad leaves; one medium tomato.

    Fruit serve examples: one apple, pear, banana or orange; two small apricots or plums; 1/4 cup fresh fruit salad; 1/4 cup stewed fruit; one cup fruit juice.

2. **Breads, cereals, pasta, and rice are high in carbohydrates and fibre.**

    Preschoolers have small stomachs and cannot eat the same amount of fibre as older children or adults. Increase fibre gradually with a variety of vegetables, fruit, breads, and cereals. Bread and cereals make tasty snacks for school children. Choose some that are whole grain.

For preschoolers: at least four servings each day.

School children: at least five servings each day; at least six for older children.

Serving size examples: one roll; a small muffin; one medium slice bread; one cup cornflakes; ½ cup muesli; 1/4 cup cooked cereal; one cup cooked pasta; one cup cooked rice; two plain sweet biscuits.

3. **Milk and milk products**

These provide protein and calcium. After two years of age, gradually introduce reduced and low-fat milk and milk products.

For preschoolers and schoolchildren: at least two to three servings each day.

Serving size examples: 250 millilitres of milk; one pot of yoghurt (125g); two slices of cheese (40 grams); 2 scoops of ice cream (140 grams).

4. **Meat and meat products; chicken; seafood; eggs; dried peas, beans, and lentils**

These foods provide protein, vitamins, and minerals, including iron and zinc.

For preschoolers and schoolchildren: at least one serving each day.

Serving size examples: *two slices cooked meat (100 grams); 3/4 cup minced or casserole meat; one egg; one medium fish fillet; 3/4 cup dried cooked beans; two chicken drumsticks.*

HEALTHY MEAL AND SNACK IDEAS

Meal	Menu	Suggestions for those with wheat/gluten dairy intolerance
Breakfast ideas	A pot of plain probiotic yoghurt (steer away from the chocolate, sweetened kinds) plus one piece of wholemeal toast with honey or Marmite, Vegemite, nut butter, or avocado and banana. Use olive or avocado oil–based spread rather than butter.	Coconut or soy yoghurt. Use spelt, rye or gluten-free bread. Use olive oil or avocado-based spreads instead of butter.
	Home-made muesli with fresh seasonal fruit (or tinned fruit in juice rather than syrup), plain probiotic yoghurt and milk.	Rice or corn-based cereals, gluten-free muesli or millet porridge with rice or almond milk.
	Creamed corn or avocado on toast with grated reduced-fat cheese (like Edam) or crumbled feta.	Soy cheese. Spelt, rye, or gluten-free bread.
	Porridge with raisins and honey cooked with milk or water. Top with stewed apple or other fruit. Add a teaspoon of flax oil.	Millet porridge.
	Wholemeal or oat muffins with pineapple and raisins	Muffins made with gluten-free flour.

	Fruit smoothie (200 millilitres of milk blended with one pot of plain acidophilus yoghurt plus two tablespoons of fruit), berries, peaches, banana, a tablespoon of a vegetable such as spinach or beetroot. Add flaxseed oil and perhaps some oats. Plus a muffin or toast	Use soy yoghurt and rice, almond, or soy milk. Spelt, rye, or gluten-free bread.
Weekend breakfasts	Cheesy scrambled eggs with toast and peach slices (or seasonal fruit).	Spelt, rye, or gluten-free bread. Soy cheese.
	Bready egg tarts (Line muffin pans with slices of bread or bacon and crack an egg into each one. Top with herbs and cheese and bake in oven for twenty minutes or until the eggs set.)	Spelt, rye, or gluten-free bread. Soy cheese.
Morning or afternoon tea	Bite-size chunks of cooked corn on the cob.	
	Plain (unbuttered and unsalted) popcorn with chocolate buttons and dried apricot pieces.	
	Fruit platters—seasonal fruit cut up into appealing bite-size pieces. Include dried apricots, prunes, and raisins (these can be soaked to make them less tough to eat). As a treat, dip fruits skewered with a cocktail stick into melted chocolate and let them harden in the fridge. Bran muffin or fruit loaf	

	Vegetable platters—seasonal raw vegetables cut into bite-size pieces: carrots, peppers, celery, broccoli, cabbage. Serve with dips: hummus (chickpea dip) or cream cheese mixed with a little sour cream and chives. For those kids that don't like their veggies, try grating carrots and cabbage mixed with a little mayonnaise or yoghurt and raisins piled onto lettuce. leaves	Omit cream cheese and sour cream. Use tahini or guacamole as a dip.
	Pikelets (thin crumpets) with low-fat cheese or a little cream cheese and pineapple, or pikelets with yoghurt, honey and berries.	Millet pancakes or a gluten-free pancakes with berries and honey or hummus and pineapple and raisins. Soy yoghurt. Use soy cheese
	Pizza slice. For fun buy (or make) small pizza bases. Add tomato puree and get kids to add their own toppings—pineapple, cheese, ham, courgettes, mushrooms, tomato. Steer away from high-fat salami, sausage, and lots of cheese.	Gluten-free pizza crust.
	Individual tubs of diced fruit and a wholemeal muffin.	Muffins made with gluten-free flour.
	Mini bagels with chocolate hazelnut spread.	Spelt, rye, or gluten-free bread.
	Rice crackers and hummus, little boxes of raisins.	

	Cold toasted sandwiches. Savoury: cheese and tomato Sweet: stewed apple and cinnamon.	Spelt, rye, or gluten-free bread. Soy cheese.
	Fruit smoothies (see breakfast).	
	Rice snacks instead of potato or corn chips.	
Packed lunch (Also see the section on lunchbox ideas)	Bread (pita bread, flatbread wraps, or burritos) with a protein filling—tuna, egg mayonnaise, cheese, cream cheese, chicken, beef, tofu, hummus. Pot of yoghurt. A piece of fruit.	Spelt, rye, or gluten-free bread. Soy cheese, hummus, or tofu soy yoghurt.
	Jacket potatoes with creamed sweetcorn and tuna or cheese and ham. Fruit jelly and piece of fruit	Soy cheese.
	Pizza slices with protein and vegetable toppings.	
	Rice salad with kidney beans, raisins. and red pepper, mixed in mayonnaise. Piece of fruit	
	Cold toasted sandwiches (see snack ideas).	
Lunch at home	See dinner ideas.	
Dinner/tea	Chicken, meat, fish, or tofu stir-fry with vegetables and noodles	
	Baked beans (low salt) or tinned spaghetti on toast.	

	Fish: Tuna pasta bake, fish pie, white fish poached in milk with cheese or a tomato-based sauce and poached cherry tomatoes. Crumbed fish and oven-baked sweet potato (kumara), parsnip, or potato chips. Serve all with favourite vegetables (frozen or fresh)	
	Homemade burgers with lamb, beef, or chicken. Serve with lettuce, pineapple, beetroot, cheese, tomato, avocado. Let children put their burgers together.	Homemade burgers (wheat-free), or veggie burgers or soy burgers. Check packages to ensure they are gluten-free.
	Sausages, potato, and kumara mash. frozen peas and corn	Soy sausages or wheat-free sausages.
	Falafels with hummus, stir-fried veggies, and brown rice.	Make sure store-bought falafels are wheat free.
	Chicken, lamb, or beef hot pot cooked with veggies.	
	Stir-fried eggy rice with vegetables and meat or tofu.	
	Beef or vegetarian lasagne.	Rice or vegetable pasta.
	Pasta ribbons with tomato or meat-based sauce with broccoli.	Rice or vegetable pasta

	Macaroni cheese with ham. Try using cottage cheese instead of hard cheese. Include veggies such as mushrooms, corn, and peppers.	Rice or vegetable pasta.
	Cottage pie—mince, grated vegetables and tomato base with a mashed potato topping.	
	Marinated chicken or salmon kebabs with ratatouille.	
Desserts	Frozen fruit yoghurt.	Coconut yoghurt.
	Carrot cake.	Gluten-free flour.
	Fruit platter.	
	Fruit crumble.	Gluten-free crumble topping.
	Custard with fruit.	Rice, soy, or almond milk.
	Fruity jelly.	
	Tinned fruit (the kind in fruit juice and not syrup) and little biscuits.	Gluten-free biscuits.
	Ice-cream and fruit.	Coconut ice-cream.
	Bread and butter pudding.	Rice, soy, or almond milk. Spelt, rye, or gluten-free bread.

THE LUNCHBOX

What we put in our children's lunchboxes has an impact on their health. Children who eat well during the day concentrate better on work and get better qualifications. Eating poorly also increases the long-term risks of diabetes and other illnesses.

As caregivers, our role is to send our kids to school with a lunchbox containing healthy foods they want to eat.

Keep it interesting

No child is going to enjoy lunch if the same thing is put in front of him or her every day. Kids often do prefer routine, so do ask them what they like and incorporate at least some of their favourite foods (perhaps modified to increase the health factor). That way, lunch is less likely to come home uneaten.

If you have a "fussy" eater, in my experience the lunch box is not the place to start experimenting or introducing new foods as it is very likely it will remain untouched and your child will be a little hungry. Leave new food introduction to times when you are around to offer guidance and positive words.

Include a variety of foods to enable your kids to get their full quota of nutrients such as carbohydrates, fats, protein, fibre, vitamins, and minerals. Variety also means a choice of textures—crunchy vegetables, foods to chew on, yoghurt, stewed fruits, and colour. Aim for orange, red, purple, and green fruits and vegetables.

What sort of lunchbox?

Use a box (not plastic) with individual compartments or a box that will fit smaller, sealed, containers. This will keep the food appealing, even towards the end of the day.

> **Handy Hint:** Put morning tea and lunch in separately labelled paper bags or boxes. Children can sometimes eat all their food at morning tea by mistake! Check whether your school is nut free before you start including peanut butter sandwiches.

Save the Planet. Use minimal or no packaging. Baking paper or waxed paper bags are more eco-friendly than plastic wrap.

What to include for lunch

As a rule of thumb, the lunchbox should contain:

- A carbohydrate such as bread, rice, or pasta (for energy) with a protein filling.

  Sandwiches are a great way to meet most lunchtime nutritional needs. For variety, use different bread types— pita pockets, flatbread (wraps), or burritos—mixed with a protein filling such as tuna, salmon, egg mayonnaise, cheese, peanut or almond butter, cottage or cream cheese, chicken, beef, tofu, or hummus. Add a little lettuce, cucumber, or carrot. Cut sandwiches into small, unusual shapes and wrap in two separate parcels so they can be unwrapped and eaten separately at different times of the day.

  Pasta or rice salad containing a tin of tuna or salmon, fresh red pepper, raisins, or corn kernels is a delicious alternative.

- A fruit or a veggie portion—a few grapes or strawberries or carrot sticks or celery.

  Provide the equivalent of one to two whole fruits or vegetables. Kids often find fruit more appealing if it is cut up for them. Try a small container of chopped seasonal fruit. Aim for those fruits that stay fresher longer.

  Boost children's veggie consumption by including carrots, celery, cucumber, or small tomatoes as a snack.

- Dairy, such as a pot of yoghurt or cubes of cheese or cream cheese in a sandwich. Avoid sweetened or flavoured yoghurt.

- A drink of water. Include a frozen or cold bottle of water to provide kids with a healthy beverage and also keep foods chilled and more appealing. Do not send juice or cordial to school.

- A healthful snack.

- Add plain biscuits such as wholemeal digestives, homemade wholemeal muffins, or a wholemeal cereal bar as a sweet, energy-giving treat.

- As a healthier alternative to potato chips, try vegetable chips, rice wheels, rice crackers, or unsweetened popcorn. Opt for the baked versions over fried versions.

- Mini boxes of raisins or dried fruit are usually a welcome snack.

Remember to pack an extra carbohydrate-rich snack if your kids are going straight from school to sports events or after-school activities to tide them over until dinnertime.

Hints for getting your kids to eat their lunch

Involve your child with lunch selections. Discuss options for the week's lunches, giving choices. Take the child shopping to choose some of the food items.

Ask your child what she likes in friends' lunches. Include one or two of these to balance with the foods that you consider important.

Include non-edible surprises in lunch boxes occasionally. Add a note, a riddle, a joke, a game, a plastic toy or puzzle. Your kids will love it; mine certainly do, and it makes me feel warm and fuzzy too.

Healthy hint: Keep portions small and provide lots of little items wrapped separately to make the food more attractive.

Check out the sugar content of muesli bars and other processed snacks. You might be surprised to see how much they contain.

Mashed avocado is a delicious and healthy spread substitute.

Check out http://www.5aday.co.nz/ for great recipes and tips to help get littlies (and adults) eating more fruit and vegetables

BOOST THEIR BRAIN POWER

When children are just starting school, the brain is processing lots of new information every day. The brain needs protein, carbohydrates, omega-3, and a range of vitamins and minerals.

What to eat to increase grey matter

- Breakfast, however big or small, gives the brain fuel with which to work. Toast, breakfast cereal, muesli, eggs, fruit, and yoghurt are all excellent ways to start the school day.

- Any protein foods—meat, fish, nuts, cheese, or milk—keep you alert. They stimulate the production of the "feel-good" hormone, dopamine, which helps your kids enjoy the subjects they like least. Peanut butter sandwiches help keep the baton passing from neuron to neuron as fast as possible. If your school does not allow peanuts, substitute egg, lean meat, or cheese. Oily fish are important for learning as well as growing. Canned fish is a healthy sandwich or wrap filler for school lunch.

- Try to add fruit and vegetables to all your child's meals to ensure a full range of mind-bending vitamins and minerals. They are also good choices for brain food snack breaks.

- Omega-3s are the brain's wonder food. Oily fish, seeds, and nuts are excellent sources of omega-3s for kids.

- No amount of the best food can replace a good night's sleep. Whether in the classroom, on the sports field, or during exams, kids will feel and do so much better if they are awake!

- Limit electronics. Research indicates that excessive use of electronics adversely affects brain health.

Chapter 4

WHEN YOUR CHILD'S EATING HABITS BECOME A PROBLEM

WHAT TO DO IF YOU HAVE A PICKY EATER

Poor nutrition can plague our children for the rest of their lives. The earlier we can start feeding our kids the right foods and setting up healthy eating habits, the better.

Do you have concerns about your child's diet and feel that he or she is not getting the best nutrition for growth and development? Does your child refuse to meals or avoid certain food groups such as vegetables? Does your child have a limited food repertoire, difficulty swallowing, or reactions to certain foods? Then, this section will assist you to understand the various causes of picky eating—both physical and behavioural—and what you can do to help your child reach her or his full potential.

On a personal note, I feel your pain if you have a child who is not eating well. My second child was also a challenge on the eating front and continues to be so! But the suggestions I give in this section can help. Keep going.

What may be causing your kid to be "fussy"?

- **The environment.** A noisy or stressful environment can be a major problem. Think about times when you have been worried or upset and how you were put off your food. It's a natural physiological response to stress.

- **Physical stuff.** Eating is the most complex, physical task humans engage in. It is the only physical task that uses all the body's organ systems—the brain and cranial nerves; heart and vascular systems; respiratory, endocrine and metabolic systems; all the muscles of the body; and the entire gastrointestinal tract! I often find that wee ones who are about to start school are still mastering the act of eating, let alone learning to use utensils properly. Perhaps your child has oral motor skill problems, such as sucking, swallowing (dysphagia), biting, chewing, or coordinating tongue movement. Or he might have fine motor skill problems. Can your child use utensils well, and grasp a drinking cup? Difficulty in these areas may lead to her to favour foods that are easy to pick up or eat over than other foods are difficult to handle.

- **Nutrition and digestive issues:** Food allergies and intolerances can cause nausea, abdominal pain, or bloating, which is bound to put anyone off food. Lack of minerals can also cause loss of appetite, poor digestion, vomiting, and reflux associated with certain foods. A relatively rare condition called childhood anorexia is characterized by extreme food refusal (eating very few or only one food or minuscule amounts of food) and loss of appetite.

- **Little or no appetite at mealtimes:** Do you have a schedule by which your child eats her meals and snacks and drinks her liquid? Does your child nibble and snack throughout the day or fill up on milk before food? If so, he may be too full at mealtimes and not eat much or any of the meal you offer. You may need to rethink the mealtime structure.

- **Overfeeding:** Does your child give clear signs that she does not want to eat? Do you recognize and respect these signs? Caregivers may need to work out why the child is not hungry at mealtimes or if you are trying to give too much food for your child's age or size.

- **Behavioural stuff:**

    Sensory processing disorder: Children with this disorder often have a difficult time touching, let alone eating food. The texture, smell, or feel of food in their hands or mouth is unpleasant to them. It is a neurological condition and should not be confused with food preferences.

    Food preferences: Minor food preferences such as preferring apples to grapes are normal and do not constitute a picky or problem eating.

    Food jags: Offering the same foods to your child day after day can lead to food jags. Food jags are periods—days or even weeks—when your child will eat only one or two foods. Food jags often occur during toddlerhood because toddlers feel comfortable with foods they know and trust. To prevent a food jag, you must rotate your child's favourite foods and continue to offer new foods. Allowing the child to continue a food jag can cause him to develop a limited food repertoire, putting him at risk for nutritional deficiencies and poor growth.

    Learned behaviour: Behaviour is linked to beliefs. Even at an early age, children can pick up cues from caregivers— vegetables are "yeuch", chocolate and ice cream are rewards for eating your meat. Check out your association with food and be careful to pass on only positive beliefs around food.

Power and control: Control is a developmental stage for two-year-olds as they realize that they can make their own decisions, and the more you try and impose rules and regulations on eating and table manners, the clearer it becomes to toddlers that the meal table is one place they can always get your attention and prompt your concern. The power and control issues can go on past the age of three, but at this age, they are also learning how to behave. Learning to sit at a table with others and using eating utensils is a difficult task, and there are many spills and messes. These mistakes are not naughtiness. Stay calm and look for opportunities to praise your child. Be uncritical. Extra attention during mealtime such as coaxing, threatening, or reasoning can unintentionally reward children for misbehaving or not eating.

The solutions: developing healthy eating habits

Solutions to environmental issues. Check the environment in which your child is eating. Provide a beautiful, quiet (no TV!), and peaceful space during mealtimes. Have your child seated when eating and drinking.

Solutions to physical issues:

Problems with eating skills. What can you do? Once a nutritionist or dietitian has completed an examination of your child and created a nutritional care plan, it may be time to visit a speech therapist for a feeding evaluation.

Problems with fine motor skills. What can you do? Improve these skills through age-appropriate toys such as puzzles, blocks, sewing, and Lego blocks. You may wish to book in with an occupational therapist.

Nutrition and digestive issues. What can you do? Have your child seen by a nutritionist to assess nutrition or digestive issues and to test for allergies or intolerances. Ensure your child is getting healthy and nutritious foods including all the food groups. Consider supplementation, which may be useful short term.

What about diminished appetite at mealtimes or consuming too much food? We need to remember that, just like adults, how much food children eat each day can vary considerably. On days when they don't eat well, parents often worry unnecessarily. A common mistake is to believe that you, the parent, knows better than your children how much they should eat. You may have in your mind a set quantity; it may be the contents of the jar you have opened, the amount of food you have lovingly prepared, or the amount another child has eaten. It may even be an educated guess based on roughly the amounts eaten over the previous few days. The snag in all this is that children's appetites vary widely from day to day, based on how they are feeling at the time.

It is so vital to respect your children's decision that they have eaten enough of what you are offering. Many problems are set up by extending the meal to coerce the child to eat more. The parent usually ends up losing. You invest time and effort with little return, and your child can become miserable and upset. If this pattern occurs repeatedly, your child will begin to associate mealtimes with stress and anxiety and will try to avoid them.

Keep an open mind about the quantity needed. Some children grow very well on much smaller amounts of food than other kids consume. Respect their decision and take the uneaten food away without showing them with body language or facial expression that you are upset or worried. In the long term, children need to learn to know when they are full. Older children who haven't learned this feeling of satiety can eat larger quantities of food than they need and may become overweight or obese. Remember to praise your child verbally and with a smile when he is eating. If he receives your attention only when he doesn't eat, then food refusal may be his way of gaining your attention.

Remember, children don't need to eat well at every meal every day. The amount of each nutrient required to keep children healthy is an average figure. Most nutrients are stored in the body, and these stores will last them some time. If they don't have milk one day, their bones will not crack up. Be satisfied that over two weeks or so, by eating more on some days and less on other days, they will be getting on average what they need. If each meal is balanced and nutritious, when they do eat well, they will be getting plenty of nutrients.

Your child might eat less than usual because she is tired. Children enjoy routine and regular mealtime. However, life does not always go to plan. In general, try and avoid meals too close to bedtime or daytime sleep. If this is unavoidable, make the meal more a quick snack and a drink of milk and give a larger meal later when they are wide awake and alert.

There are too many distractions. If you are out, children may be more curious about their new environment or the people around them than the meal. One lost meal won't matter, and they will probably eat more at the next meal that you offer on familiar ground.

Your child is not so feeling so flash. Insisting he try to eat will make him more miserable and may put him off the food you are attempting to feed. An association with the food and feeling sad may be established.

Your child may not enjoy the meal. Children's taste buds are sensitive and change with time. You may be offering food that they have enjoyed in the past, but they have now become bored with. Perhaps provide two courses: a savoury course followed by a pudding. This gives them two chances to eat sufficient calories and nutrients. Make sure desserts are nutritious, based on some fruit and containing other ingredients such as milk and/or eggs.

Sheena's Words of Wisdom: Strategies for Varying your Child's Diet

The one thing I can offer as a parent as well as a health professional is that sometimes there seems to be no rhyme or reason to a child not eating well. While my first child, Dylan, was a breeze when it came to eating well—loving veggies, eating most anything in front of him—James was a different story. If we had left James to it, he wouldn't have eaten any vegetables apart from carrots and green beans, and his only protein intake would have been sausages. Honestly, we could not work out what the issue was. However, after using the ideas that follow, we now have a healthy young boy who consumes a varied repertoire of foods. The key things for us were persistence and providing clarity around what we expected without drama. We are still working on tomatoes and spinach. It may take a few years, but we will get there.

What can you do if your child is not eating?

- **Try to remain calm and don't feel it is your fault.** There are many reasons that some children do not enjoy eating. It may be related to something that happened when they were very young over which you had no control. You may never know the reason that food is less enjoyable to them than it is to others.

- **Set up rules around food and eating for your house.** Discuss mealtime rules with your children: "In our house we ..." and stick to the rules. Ask children to tell you the rules before mealtimes. Calmly remind them if they don't remember.

- **Always talk about food positively.** Little ears hear everything.

- **Get your kids involved in shopping, preparation, and cooking.** One sure way to get kids interested in eating well is to include them in the whole process from an early age. Even two-year-olds can mix the muffin batter, shred some lettuce, or arrange a cut tomato on a plate. Older kids can help make snacks like muffins and muesli slices. They can put together their burgers themselves, add toppings to a pizza, and decorate fairy cakes. Once they are old enough to cook a meal for themselves or the family—from simple beans on toast to a more challenging apple crumble—let children find shopping items for you at the supermarket. Ask their advice on which foods to buy—berries or peaches, spaghetti ribbons or twirls. And let them help unpack and put away the shopping. Give them responsibilities around setting the table.

  Note: ensure your child is not in any danger—hot elements, boiling water, knives, mixing blades, and other hazards are always present around food.

- **Be prepared.** Busy working parents? Then put aside time at the weekend or evenings to prepare and freeze meals for the week. Go shopping at least once a week to ensure the pantry is full. Think about what healthy breakfast, snack, and dinner ingredients to buy before you go. Get up half an hour earlier to prepare lunches and snacks, or better still, get your children to clear away breakfast while you make them.

- **Get into a mealtime routine.** Regular family mealtimes, including morning and afternoon snacks, will help kids to pick up good eating habits. As well, these are excellent opportunities to encourage family members to communicate with each other. If breakfast is usually a rush, try getting everyone up half an hour earlier so you can all eat at the table and not on the run. All meals should be eaten sitting down at the table—even snacks.

- **Make mealtimes a social occasion.** The family can have fun eating and chatting together. Children may lose their appetite if they are shouted at, coerced to eat more food when they have had enough or dislike the food, are continually offered food throughout the day, or are rushed.

- **Provide a variety of foods**. No child is going to enjoy food if the same old thing is put in front of her every day. Variety also enables your kids to get their full quota of nutrients such as carbohydrates, fats, protein, fibre, vitamins, and minerals. Variety also means a range of textures—crunchy vegetables, foods to chew on, custards, stewed fruits. Variety also offers colour—aim for orange, red, purple, and green fruits and vegetables. Plan several different meal ideas and foods each day to keep them interested in healthy eating and to maintain or achieve health and vitality, today and long after they have left the nest.

- **Give your child choices**. For example, does he want his veggies raw or cooked? Which two vegetables would she like tonight? Does he want his sandwich cut into squares or triangles? Does she want Marmite or honey on her toast? How much does he want on his plate? Does she want mashed or whole potatoes?

- **Make sure each meal is balanced and nutritious.** This way, when your child does eat, she will get plenty of nutrients.

- **Make it taste good**. You will be surprised how kids take to herbs and spices as flavourings. Try mild chilli or curry powders. Garlic, cinnamon, basil, parsley, coriander, and a host of other flavourings can take the place of butter, tomato sauce, and other processed sauces. Do not salt food—use lemon salt (citric acid) as an alternative.

- **Offer small portions.** This will prevent kids from feeling overwhelmed by large plates of food. Praise them when they finish; offer a little more but don't insist they eat more.

- **Some children find it easier to drink than eat.** If kids fill up on large quantities of fluid, there is no room left for food in their small stomachs. Give all drinks in cups and limit drinks between meals to water. Don't give any fluid for half an hour or so before or after a meal.

- **Mix food favourites with foods that are not so popular.** Introduce vegetables as a component of a recipe; for example, add grated carrot to meat hot pot or peas to potato fritters.

- **Ensure kids aren't filling up with junky snack foods before meals.** This is a sure way to encourage kids to reject those beautiful meals you have cooked for them. Offer food at regular meals and one small snack halfway between meals. The rest of the time, don't offer any food. Don't give sweets and chocolates "just so that they have eaten something".

- **Try not to rush meals.** Do not extend a mealtime in the hope your child will eat more. Limit mealtimes to twenty to thirty minutes and take away uneaten food without comment. Wait for the next snack or meal when your child may eat more. Note: if the meal isn't eaten, do not offer alternatives. Say something like, "I see you are not hungry at the moment. I will put the food away in a special container, and you can have it later."

- **Change the venue of meals.** This might be an impromptu picnic with everyone in the garden or on the playroom floor. Make it fun!

- **Set a good example.** Remember, children learn by copying, so eat with your children as often as possible. Show them that you find eating fun and pleasurable.

- **Don't use food as a bribe or reward.** If you offer food B as a reward for eating up food A, you are telling them that food B is a yummy food and food A is not so hot—usually the opposite to the health message you have in your mind.

- **Make the transition from junk food grazing to structured and healthy meals.** For obvious reasons, we need to encourage our children to eat wholesome foods rather than takeaways and processed foods. If your child is overdoing the junk food, here is a way you might want to tackle the transition to healthy eating with your kids.

Explain why some not-so-healthy foods they have regularly been eating now need to become treats. Explain in a positive and motivational way that will appeal to them—tell them they will be more likely to make the school team, stop getting sick, run faster, have more energy, do well at school, get fitter. Then make a deal with the child. Write down these guidelines:

- How many treats they can have a week

- What constitutes a treat (for example: one bag of chips, one pie, one can of fizzy drink, one ice-cream)

- When the treats can be eaten: (for example, Friday night while watching a movie, a special treat for school lunch midweek, or an ice cream with a friend on Saturday afternoon)

Write the agreement as a contract and both sign it. Involve your child in the transaction process. Make sure they understand why these foods are now treats so they do not feel they are being punished or feel humiliated. Note: A star, or tick chart is a fabulous idea. Once a child has gained a certain number of star stickers over time (ideally a week), he or she is offered a non-food reward. Agree with the reward and time at the start of the contract.

Most children will get an adequate intake of the foods they need, but for some youngsters, getting good nutrition can become a long-term problem that can affect growth, performance, and mental health. If you are at all worried, keep a written record of what your child is eating for a few days (without her knowing). Usually, you will find she is getting enough—but if you are still worried, talk to a dietitian, nutritionist, or other health professional.

WHAT TO DO IF YOUR CHILD IS OVEREATING

One in ten Kiwi kids aged five to fourteen is overweight or obese, and although the stats vary from country to country, most of us realize that excessive body weight is a massive worldwide problem for both kids and adults. The scary thing is that most cases of childhood obesity start in our under-fives, and 80 per cent of obese kids will become obese adults. We need to prioritize prevention in the early years.

We must remember that obesity is a medical condition that can affect our children physically, mentally, and emotionally. Obesity can lead to some serious medical issues—type 2 diabetes, high blood pressure, poor wound healing, kidney disease, fatty liver, recurring chest infections, bowlegs, difficulty breathing during sleep, asthma, depression, and more. Not only that, but there is also the social stigma and bullying. We know how cruel both kids and adults can be.

But how do you know if your child is bigger than he or she should be, and what can you do about it?

Although there is heaps of public awareness about the issue, it seems many caregivers don't recognize their children are too heavy for their health. A recent New Zealand survey shows that over half of parents with obese children believed that their children were a healthy weight. Also, nine out of ten parents of overweight children aged two to four years thought that their children were a normal weight. Studies around the world show similar results.

It seems that, because so many people—adults and children—are now too heavy, we have stopped noticing fatness. Obesity has become normalized! We don't see our kiddies as oversized because many of their friends are the same. And who wants to acknowledge our children are overweight? Then we'll have to deal with all baggage that comes with that!

The first thing we need to know is how big is too big? The body mass index (BMI) is an easy way to check if a child is too heavy for his or her height. You can find a BMI calculator online or use the following equation to measure BMI:

BMI = weight (kilograms) divided by height in metres squared

By plotting your child's BMI value on a BMI chart, you can see how your child compares with other children of the same age and gender. Ask your health professional for the chart you should use, or use the charts put out by your country's health department.

If you use a chart:

- BMI-for-age from the fifth percentile to less than the eighty-fifth percentile means a healthy weight.

- BMI-for-age from the eighty-fifth percentile to less than the ninety-fifth percentile means the child is overweight (an approximate BMI of 25+).

- BMI-for-age greater than the ninety-fifth percentile means the child is obese (an approximate BMI of 30).

BMI is a rough guide best used to measure the whole population rather than individuals and is only one measure of obesity. Because there is such a wide range of heights and weights for each age, the measure can be inaccurate for some children. Also, some kids going through a growth spurt may be within the healthy weight range one day and next month could be in the overweight range. Additionally, body fat changes with age and is different for each gender—that is why the charts are age and gender specific.

Every child in New Zealand is provided with a Well Child Tamariki Ora "My Health Book". The book has a section in which your child's health is monitored and recorded, including height and weight. If you are concerned, then it is well worth plotting your kid's measurements on the chart regularly. In New Zealand, it becomes tricky after the age of five when Plunket (health) nurse visits finish and it's up to parents to monitor their children. That's where a long piece of wood on which you can record your kid's height and weight comes in handy. You can then use a BMI calculator to check all is okay.

What to do if you are worried

If you suspect your child is overweight and seems to have a high BMI, then it is time to visit a doctor, dietitian, or registered nutritionist. When parents bring their kids to me, they often get quite emotional. They have acknowledged there is a possible problem, and suddenly the weight is lifted off their shoulders. They breathe a sigh of relief and feel there is hope now that they can start to work with professionals to come up with an action plan and improve the situation.

But trying to lose weight is far tougher than preventing your child from becoming fat in the first place. Prevention is the key. As soon as you notice your child is putting on the kilos, it's time to spring into action.

Why are our kids getting fatter?

The single biggest problem is our children's diet. Genetic variables, being big-boned, and increased use of electronics causing lack of physical exercise are factors to consider, but junk food intake is the biggest problem.

Many studies and surveys over the years have shown that behaviours such as physical inactivity, missing breakfast, missing lunch, buying food to eat at school from the corner or school shop, drinking fizzy drinks, watching TV, and excessive time on electronics are responsible for the obesity epidemic.

The World Health Organization (WHO) states that obesity is due to a child's exposure to an unhealthy lifestyle (the obesogenic environment) combined with the biological and behavioural changes due to this environment. These responses vary depending on the norms of the child's family, community, and culture. WHO also suggests that obesity risk can pass from one generation to the next as children inherit socioeconomic status and cultural norms, including family eating and physical activity behaviours. As we talked about earlier, in some cultures and parts of the world, overweight and obesity are becoming social norms.

Governments and health bodies are working hard to beat the child (and adult) obesity epidemic. Strategies include:

- Education about nutrition during pregnancy

- Restricting junk food marketing to children

- Introducing a sugar tax

- Introducing policies on the types of foods and drinks allowed in schools

- New physical activity programmes

Additionally, we should all consider what we can do in our own families and communities to help keep our country and world healthy and happy.

It takes a village to raise a child

It seems sad to me that many of our communities don't work together to raise their children. New mums come to me because they have been diagnosed with postnatal depression and they truly have no one to reach out to outside their immediate family. Or I witness overweight or struggling children who are bullied or ostracized, and no one says a thing or checks in to see if they are okay.

My question is, how would life be different for our kids if we did support each other more? Would things improve if we were more courageous and voiced our concerns and offered help for an overweight, sad, or bullied child, an elderly neighbour, or depressed new mum? What do you think?

It may not be your child who is having weight or health issues, but if we all help each other to raise our children, then not only will our wee ones flourish, but our communities will become more healthy and connected.

Making changes

What sort of things might make a difference?

- Provide caregivers with a copy of this book to help them to understand what is needed to keep our kids healthy and well.

- If you are holding a party or community event, then encourage water or milk as the drink of choice over the sugary pop varieties.

- Have you been asked to sell biscuits, sugary drinks, or chocolate to raise funds? Then suggest an alternative or refuse. Explain that you won't sell products that encourage obesity or sickness. Carry this campaign to the school parent-teacher association (PTA).

- Start a nutrition group in your community. Invite your local health professional along to speak about diet, wellness, activity, and anti-bullying.

- Get your school or community to support local or international programmes aimed at teaching kids to eat well and be active.

- You can't out-exercise a poor diet. A balance between good nutrition and adequate activity is the key.

- Say no to the offer of lollies from hairdressers, shop owners, and so on. Suggest they offer more healthful rewards if they feel the need.

- Ensure that your children and their friends spend most of the time playing actively outdoors with just half or hour or so of downtime on the electronics.

- Let a friend or school mum know that you are concerned about her child's weight and ask if you can do anything to help.

The NZ Nutrition Foundation (www.nutritionfoundation.org.nz) offers the following useful advice.

Losing weight too quickly can leave your child short of vitamins and minerals, which can lead to reduced growth long term. As a parent, you have a role in shaping your child's dietary habits. You can control what, when, and how your child eats, as well as being a role model. Help your child learn healthy, lifelong habits through good family eating patterns and meal structure as well as keeping active.

Get active

Here are some tips on establishing good exercise habits:

- Encourage your children to be active for about an hour a day. Making it fun and being active with them will help keep your children motivated, and they will see it as an enjoyable part of their day rather than a punishment.

- Choose something they enjoy—from team sports to playground games, or even dancing. Walking or biking to school is also a great way to be active without having to find extra time in the day—and it's free. Some schools have a walking school bus programme in which adults walk children to school.

- Create a healthy environment for your family by limiting time spent in front of the TV, game consoles, and computers (outside school) to a maximum of two hours per day. Less time in front of a screen gives kids more time to be active.

- The best way to cut down energy (kilojoules/calories) is by eating smaller amounts. Don't try to change too many foods at once. Build small changes into your children's everyday habits.

- Regular meals help prevent your children from getting hungry. Always start the day with breakfast, such as a couple of slices of toast or a bowl of cereal along with a piece of fruit and a glass of milk.

- Choose lite and trim (skinny) milk instead of regular full-fat milk for everyone in the family over two years of age.

- When using cheese, choose lower-fat cheese varieties such as Edam or low-fat versions of cream cheese, cottage cheese, and sour cream instead of tasty, Colby, or mild cheeses.

- Make healthy choices easy by making fresh fruit and vegetables readily available for snacks. Chopping fruit into small pieces can help make them more manageable for children.

- As children grow older, change from white to whole grain bread, as these are more filling and contain more nutrients.

- Limit biscuits, crisps, fried foods, and fizzy drinks as these are high in energy, fat, and sugar. Try choosing the smallest option of these foods; for example, a snack-sized bag of crisps, a mini chocolate bar, or a limit of one chocolate biscuit.

- Water and low-fat milk should be the drinks offered to children. Try keeping water chilled in the fridge for a more refreshing drink.

- The Feeding Our Families website has many useful tips: www.feedingourfamilies.org.nz

Most of the ideas I've listed here don't cost a lot of money—just a few minutes or hours of your time and loads of giving and love.

Chapter 5

BEING IN ACTION— IN A SUPERHERO KIND OF WAY

GET MOVING! BE ACTIVE EVERY DAY!

Just like an unused bike may become rusty, our muscles and bones need to be kept working so they don't cease up. Activity is necessary to keep our children's bones strong and their hearts pumping, not to mention it's great for weight maintenance, balancing mood, and sleeping well. It can also be good fun for everyone in the family. Some of the best, most connected times I have had with my children were trekking in the forest, playing cricket on the beach, or even romping through a game of Twister in the living room. (We are all just hopeless because we laugh so much!).

Play doesn't just keep children active—it helps them develop socially, emotionally, and cognitively.

Whilst doing research for this book, I found that some of the most valuable information came from the New Zealand Ministry of Health (check out http://www.health.govt.nz/our-work/prevenative-health-wellness/physical-activity#kids), who recommend that our children "sit less, move more, sleep well". They suggest that our young people should be active at home, at school, and at play during the weekends and in the community.

Our kids need to do at least one hour of moderate or vigorous physical activity spread over the day. It may be just walking or biking to and from school and running up the stairs. Games like tag, skipping, and soccer at break times are good for giving the body a workout. Swimming is both fun and fabulous for keeping our kids well.

The challenge I find most parents face is enticing kids away from the keyboard and getting them outside. Unfortunately, it is our responsibility as caregivers to be the "mean electronics police" and limit time in front of computers, the television, and games consoles.

So how do we get our kids to become superheroes instead of super sloths?

Earlier in the book, I talked about making sure that we motivate and encourage our kids by getting into their world. Your children are not going to be particularly excited if you tell them that exercise will help their bowel motions or give them the opportunity to live until they are over a hundred years old. Getting them excited about being as strong or bendy as their favourite hero or as fast as the local sports star they admire is much more compelling and relevant.

Here are a few more tips to getting your kids off the couch.

- **Set a good example.** Be physically active yourself. Of course, it means you are reaping the benefits too as you look after your own health and wellness as well as connecting with your puppies

- **Start slowly.** If your child is not usually active, start with five to ten minutes of easy activity a day and increase that time a little each week. Aim to build up to at least one hour of exercise each day—you can spread that hour over the day.

  For example:

  o Instead of getting in the car for short trips, try walking, biking, or scooting with your children. Start by doing this once a week and add more trips over time.

- o Try setting up a walking school bus with other families or use the one available at your school

- o Encourage your children to play outside as much as possible, including during breaks at school.

- o Encourage your children to join a school sports team, local sports club, dance group, scouts, or another active group.

- o Try to do something fun and energetic as a family each weekend such as going on beach or forest walks, building a den in the woods, kicking a ball outside, playing tennis or netball, or flying a kite.

- **Limit Screen time.** Cut down the amount of time your under-five children spend watching TV or sitting in front of a computer screen to less than one hour a day (outside school time). From my experience, not only does excess electronic time lead to less activity (apart from arm and finger action!), but kids are also more likely to be munching on calorie-laden, nutrient-poor snacks during that time.

- **Keep moving.** Encourage kids to break up their sitting time. Let's say they are drawing or making models at the table. Try getting them to stand up as they work, which encourages more moving about.

- **Encourage active playdates.** It's much more fun to keep fit with friends. Invite children around and play hide and seek in the garden or around the house. Visit the skate park or beach. Throw a few hoops at the local school or visit the local swimming pool.

Here are a heap more activity ideas:

Aerobic activities that increase the heart rate and keep kids fit.		
Moderate-intensity activities make kids breathe harder, and their hearts beat faster.	**Vigorous-intensity activities** make kids puffed, so they can't say more than a few words without pausing for breath.	**Muscle-strengthening activities** build strength in the muscles, tendons, and ligaments. They improve joint function and reduce the risk of injury.
Cycling Rollerblading Skateboarding Brisk walking Dancing Games that require catching and throwing (like T-ball or softball)	Active games—running and chasing games like tag or Frisbee Cycling Skipping Martial arts like karate Running Sports like football, netball, rugby, touch rugby, swimming, hockey Dancing Bouncing on a trampoline	Games like tug-of-war Rope and tree climbing or climbing walls Yoga Swinging on playground equipment and bars

My two children are totally different in temperament, interests, and even which types of activities they like to do. This can be interesting, to say the least, when it comes to finding family activities that engage us all. We also have the added challenge of a four-year age gap, and so competency is also something we take into consideration. All I can say it is that it's doable if you get creative. Let's say we are going for a Sunday-morning mountain bike ride. We all do a couple of family rides together, and then my daredevil husband and our older boy go and thrash some crazy rides while my younger son and I battle out some more relaxed tracks. It works, and we are all happy and keeping fit. What sort of things might work in your household?

Chapter 6

A FOCUS ON YOUR CHILD'S MENTAL AND EMOTIONAL NEEDS

The complex brain

The human brain contains around 86 billion neurons and 86 trillion connections between these neurons; that is more connections than there are stars in the Milky Way galaxy or any galaxies in the known universe. The human brain is one of the most complex and wondrous things we know of, and it is the product over three and a half billion years of evolution. There is much we can do to look after our children's brains and the associated cognitive function, learning ability, mood, and emotions. A healthy mind is essential for a healthy, happy life.

NERVOUS SYSTEM DISORDERS AND BEHAVIOURAL ISSUES

I often ask parents if they have noticed if their child started behaving "badly" because of something going on in the household. Most often they will either agree that is true *or* they may not have even noticed a change in behaviour. I know for a fact that, as my children were growing up from toddlers to pre-schoolers, they were sensitive to whether I was present with them; that is, I was eager to engage with them rather than just physically in the room with my thoughts elsewhere. What we must recognize is that our children have feelings and emotions that need nourishing daily, just as their physical bodies require nourishment. And "nourishment" not only includes good food and exercise; it also means feeding them an abundance of love and hugs and connection as well as mental stimulation.

Let's check out why things may not be going so well with your wee one's mental or emotional health and what actions we can take to get things back on track.

The stressed and anxious child

Most of us would like to believe that our kids are leading stress-free and cruisy lives. They don't have to hold down a job or pay the mortgage, do they! However, in this day and age, the stresses our children face can be enormous:

- Some kids are overly busy with activities five to seven days a week, from sports practices and games to drama and music lessons. Today the number of extracurricular activities available to those who can afford them is phenomenal. However, too much scheduled time means too little time for creative play and relaxation.

- When kids overhear adult conversations or the world news headlines, they can start to get anxious about things like Grandma's health issues or terrorist attacks. The boundaries between what used to be considered adult information and entertainment now seems blurred in many Westernized cultures, mainly because of easier access to information through the internet and TV.

- Tension in the house can affect children. If you and your partner are going through a sticky patch or are discussing a separation or financial worries, the negative emotions can affect your little ones.

- Children often have issues with friendships or bullying at school.

What can we do?

- Ask yourself and your child if it would be worthwhile to cut down on extracurricular activities to see how that helps. Or arrange the times so that the child has more free days to relax and engage in free play.

- Ensure that your kids hear only information that is not going to make them anxious or upset. If they do need to know something unhappy, such as the death of a family member or pet, then remember to phrase the news in the least surprising way. With regards to world news, you may feel it is important for them to know what is happening outside your country. If you do, it would be worth sitting down with them and talking through the news so you can help them to understand what is going on and give them the space to ask questions and voice their concerns.

- Ensure you know what your child is viewing on computers and TV. Wherever possible, make sure you can see and hear what they are watching. You can put some simple cybersecurity steps in place, locking access to inappropriate material and password protecting your own devices. Look online for more ways to keep children cyber safe. ⸱

- Are you getting divorced or separated? Then ensure the children are not made to take sides or to listen to negative comments by one parent about the other. Ensure they know it is not their fault.

Sheena's Words of Wisdom: Listen to Your Kids

Please listen to their concerns and validate what they are saying; something that may seem minor to you may seem humungous to your child, especially if he or she has not grasped a true or full story. Our role is to listen and understand their anxieties.

Of course, a child's anxiety can be due to—or exacerbated by—poor diet, poor digestion, immune imbalance, and modern-day toxic threats from air, food, water, and soil pollution. Unborn children, babies, and young children are the most vulnerable to these types of risks. Because they are smaller, they may consume or take in more pollutants per unit of body weight. Additionally, their organs and blood/brain barrier are still developing and are more sensitive or porous to toxins. Toxins from many different areas can all affect our kids' health—food additives; chemicals and pesticides in and on our foods; chemical-laden lotions, shampoos and body washes; car emissions.

How can we reduce the toxic load?

- **Minimize toxic exposure.** Choose household cleaning and washing products and personal hygiene products such as body washes and shampoos that don't contain nasty chemicals. Better still, make your own from essential oils and other natural ingredients and save money and the planet in the process. There are lots of websites that offer organic or eco-friendly ingredients, recipes, or products.

- **Aim to cook from scratch.** Whenever possible, avoid additive laden processed foods.

- **Eat organic.** Buy organic whenever possible. If organic produce isn't available, wash fruits and vegetables thoroughly to get rid of as many pesticide residues as possible.

- **Drink clean, filtered tap water.** Skip the bottled water to decrease your exposure to BPA. BPA stands for bisphenol A, an industrial chemical found in polycarbonate plastics and epoxy resins. Polycarbonate plastics are often used in containers that store food and beverages, such as water and other consumer goods. Some research has shown that BPA can seep into food or drinks from containers that are made with BPA and cause adverse health effects.

Feed your brain. What nutrients support a healthy mind and emotions?

Earlier in the book, we talked about foods and nutrients that feed the brain (see "Boost Their Brainpower" in chapter 3). If we take this further, we find that there is loads of research that indicates that kids who eat a typical Western diet high in refined sugar and carbohydrates and processed foods are more likely to suffer from depression and anxiety, and they do not do so well a school. A diet high in vegetables, fruits, unprocessed grains, and fish and seafood, and containing little or no processed and refined foods and sugars and modest amounts of lean meats and dairy is the way to go.

Why is that the case? The biological pathways that link diet and health include inflammation, oxidative stress, and the gut microbiome. This has been known for ages. Extensive evidence now also shows the importance of the hippocampus in the association between nutrition and mental and cognitive health. The hippocampus is part of the brain associated with learning and memory as well as mood regulation.

The gut-brain connection. Looking after your digestive health is vital for brain health. Did you know that about 95 per cent of your serotonin, a neurotransmitter that helps regulate sleep and appetite and moods and inhibits pain, is produced in your gut? Also, the function of the hundred million nerve cells or neurons that line your gut is influenced by the "good" bacteria that make up your intestinal microbiome. We talked about this in the digestive health section of the book, but importantly, the nerve cells activate neural pathways that travel directly between the gut and the brain via the vagus nerve.

Once again, foods containing probiotics such as plain yoghurt, and fermented foods such as sauerkraut, miso, and kombucha will benefit your child. Check out microbiome-enhancing foods in chapter 3. A probiotic and prebiotic supplement may also help.

Eat loads of good fats. Foods such as omega-3 fatty acids, found in fish; flavonoids; antioxidant-rich berries; and resveratrol, a polyphenol found in red grapes and other fruits as well as nuts and seeds, stimulate neurogenesis, reduce oxidative activity, and down-regulate the pro-inflammatory processes.

DOES YOUR KID NEED MORE ZZZZS?

I am often asked how much sleep is the right amount for a child. This is a fundamental question; in fact, sleep and lack of it is a topic that comes up time and time again at lifestyle and medicine conferences I attend. The importance of sleep has well been known since the start of time, but more and more evidence backs up its part in weight control, heart health, mood balance, sugar balance, and more. The quality and quantity of your child's sleep are just as important because sleep has a direct impact on your child's mental and physical development.

The importance of sleep

Every living creature needs to sleep. It is the primary activity of the brain during early development. The sleep-wake cycle, or circadian rhythm, is regulated by light and dark, and this rhythm takes time to develop, which is why new-borns have irregular sleep schedules. The rhythms begin to develop at about six weeks, and most infants have a regular sleep cycle by three to six months. By the age of two, most children will have spent more time asleep than awake.

There are two alternating types of sleep:

- **Rapid eye movement (REM)** is also known as "active" sleep. During REM sleep, our brains are active, and dreaming occurs. Breathing and heart rates are irregular, and our bodies don't move.

- **Non-rapid eye movement (NREM)** is also known as "quiet" sleep. During this deep sleep state, blood supply to the muscles increases, tissue growth and repair occur, hormones are released for growth and energy, and energy is restored.

Pre-schoolers typically sleep eleven to thirteen hours each night, and most do not nap after five years of age. As with toddlers, difficulty falling asleep and waking up during the night are common. At this age, our kids are developing their imaginations, and pre-schoolers may experience night-time fears and nightmares. Also, sleepwalking and sleep terrors peak during the preschool years.

Sleep tips for pre-schoolers

- Maintain a regular and consistent sleep schedule.

- Establish a relaxing bedtime routine that ends in the room where the child sleeps. Start early with a relaxing bath or shower and then spend time reading a book. Remember to choose books with relaxing topics. (It's not a good idea to be reading about monsters under the bed in the evenings!) Then teeth and bed. Lavender oil in the bath or dabbed on their feet before bed is a beautiful way to help relaxation. Otherwise, for a child who finds it hard to sleep, doing some gentle breathing or mindfulness exercises can help.

- Your child should sleep in the same sleeping environment every night, in a room that is cool, quiet, and dark—and without a TV or any electronics.

FUN MINDFULNESS ACTIVITIES FOR KIDS

Mindfulness is using the five senses— sight, smell, touch, feel, listening—to engage in the world around you, both physically and non-judgmentally. If you are anything like me, I am on a permanent quest to be more mindful because I know how good it makes me feel. If you have a child who is anxious, or has difficulty calming down, building a mindfulness practise might be beneficial.

Mindfulness techniques can be wonderfully empowering for your children. They can help them better self-regulate, manage stress and anxiety, and have more compassion for themselves and others. Research has also indicated that mindfulness is a way of treating children (and adolescents) who live with conditions such as attention deficit (hyperactivity) disorders, autism spectrum disorder (ASD), and depression.

And it doesn't need to be a chore. Any activity can be done with a sense of mindfulness, even eating as a family. You can teach your kids to pay attention to the colours, smell, and textures of the components of their meals and to think about how the food may be nurturing them and keeping them healthy.

How do you explain mindfulness to your kids? The experts suggest you don't need to explain; rather, invite your children to *feel* it first. You might start by showing them how to pay attention to their breath and the stillness between the out breath and in breath. Explain that this quiet place is always with us—when we are angry, frightened, happy, or excited, and so they can choose to learn to come back to this tranquil space at any time.

Here are some fun mindfulness tools that you can teach your children:

- **Take ten breaths**: Practicing mindful breathing is a simple and effective way to help children calm their bodies and be "present". Try this one at bedtime once your child is lying down and ready to go to sleep.

  Take ten deep breaths together. Ask your child to close her eyes and put her hand (or her favourite soft toy) on her belly. Ask her to breathe in so that the air fills her tummy (just like filling a balloon with air). Show her how to breathe out slowly. If ten breaths are too many, start with five and work your way up together with practice.

- **Notice three things**: Taking a moment to notice the world around you can help bring you back to the present, especially when you're overwhelmed by stress or emotion. You can practice noticing three things you see, hear, or feel through touch to help you be present.

  Sit down with your child wherever you are and tell him you want to show him the "notice three things" game. Look around and tell him three things you see. Then let him have a turn. Then move to three things you hear and three things you feel (for example, feeling your feet touching the ground).

After you play, explain that this can be a helpful game to play with you or by himself if he's ever feeling anxious or upset.

I find this has helped me appreciate things around me much more—from the multitude of colours of leaves on the trees to the wonderful feeling of a child's hug.

- **Draw your emotions:** Young children sometimes have difficulty naming or describing their feelings, but a drawing can express emotions without words. Drawing can be a great way for a child to pay attention to what she's feeling at a given moment.

  Get some paper and crayons, pop on some relaxing music, and then ask her to close her eyes and notice how she is feeling. She can then draw the feeling. You can also draw how you are feeling. If she wishes to, she can name the emotion.

There are plenty more exercises to check out on the internet. The more we and our children practice, the more aware we become of ourselves and the environment around us. And the more we develop an appreciation of everyday life. The concept of mindfulness can sound daunting, but have some fun and know that, by teaching this technique to your child, you're providing valuable life-long skills.

ATTENTION DEFICIT (HYPERACTIVITY) DISORDERS—TIPS FOR AVOIDING LEARNING DIFFICULTIES LATER

Attention deficit hyperactivity disorder (ADHD) and attention deficit disorder (ADD) are neurological and behaviour-related conditions that cause difficulty in concentrating as well as impulsiveness and excessive energy.

Individuals with ADHD symptoms find concentrating challenging, and they have difficulty sitting still. Those with ADHD are typically more disruptive than individuals with ADD.

New Zealand statistics and information:

- ADHD affects 2 to 5 per cent of all children.

- ADHD was first described a hundred years ago but is no more prevalent now; it's just better recognized.

- Although up to three times as many boys are diagnosed with ADHD as girls, it is suspected that the incidence is more like 1:1.

- Research suggests that 50 to 80 per cent of children with ADHD will continue to meet diagnostic criteria in adolescence, and 50 to 70 per cent will have symptoms that cause impairment as adults.

- The incidence of ADHD is approximately the same across all countries and races.

- Most children who have ADHD have the social and emotional maturity of children two-thirds their age.

- The stimulants methylphenidate (brand name Ritalin), dextroamphetamine and amphetamine (brand name Adderall), and dextroamphetamine (brand name Dexedrine) have been used for over forty years. Between 80 and 90 per cent of children with significant ADHD are helped in the short term by one of these stimulants.

- Approximately half of the children who present with ADHD are also troubled by specific learning disabilities such as dyslexia.

- Oppositional defiant disorder, which typically causes defiant and disobedient behaviour towards authority figures, is a co-morbid condition found in 40 to 60 per cent of children with ADHD

- Recent research suggests that sleep deprivation, circadian rhythm disturbances, and sleep-disordered breathing (including mouth breathing) may lead to the induction of ADHD-like symptoms.

Researchers suggest that the long-term consequences of ADHD include dire psychological, educational, and psychiatric outcomes. Early diagnosis and intervention are essential factors in preventing the debilitating effects of this condition.

Symptoms of ADD and ADHD

The intensity of these symptoms can vary significantly from individual to individual, depending on environment, diet, and other factors. Children may exhibit one or more of the following symptoms of ADHD and ADD:

- Difficulty in concentrating and diminished focus

- Easily distracted

- Easily bored

- Difficulty organizing or completing tasks

- Prone to losing things

- Doesn't listen

- Problems following instructions

- Fidgety behaviour, squirming

- Extremely challenged at being still or quiet

- Impatient

Adults may exhibit one or more of the following symptoms of ADD and ADHD:

- Difficulty focusing and concentrating on a task, project, or conversation

- Overwhelming emotional and physical restlessness

- Frequent mood swings

- Prone to anger and a hot temper

- Disorganized

- Low tolerance of people, situations, and surroundings

- Unstable relationships

- Increased risk for addiction

The most common treatments of ADD and ADHD today are medications that have been linked to suicidal thoughts and personality changes. These central nervous system stimulants can cause nervousness, agitation, anxiety, insomnia, vomiting, increased heart rate, increased blood pressure, and even psychosis.

With these side effects, it is easy to see why so many people are seeking effective natural solutions. The good news is that natural treatments that are both effective and do not cause the possible side effects of prescription medications.

The primary way the natural medical model differs from the orthodox medical model is that we seek to find and treat the *cause* rather than the *symptoms*.

Root causes of ADD and ADHD

According to several international studies, root causes may increase the risk and, in many cases, worsen the symptoms:

- A genetic link

- Environmental factors such as electromagnetic fields (EMF)

- Diet and nutrient deficiencies—refined sugar, artificial sweeteners, and chemical food additives, nutritional deficiencies, preservatives, and food allergies

- In children, a lack of interest

- Learning style (Some children learn better by seeing or doing—kinesthetic learning—rather than by hearing. Differing needs may not be catered for, or even understood in a traditional learning environment, which makes successful education tricky for all involved.)

The natural and biomedical approach to ADD and ADHD

The aim is to address the underlying metabolic, digestive, and immunological factors that may contribute to the neurological symptoms. By addressing these, we aim to reduce the severity of symptoms as well as the impact on the lives of the individuals, their family members, and carers. Here are the five key principles:

1. Dietary intervention to help correct nutritional imbalances, resolve gut dysbiosis, and heal the gut wall enabling normal gut function

(including nutrient absorption and reduction of food toxins that affect brain health)

2. Digestive tract healing

3. Nutritional medicine to balance biochemistry and deficiencies and to target oxidative stress and inflammation

4. Detoxification - promotion of methylation, sulfation (biological processes that may be not work optimally in individuals with ADHD or ADD), and clearance of heavy metals (which may be elevated in those with ADHD and ADD).

5. Neurodevelopment and behavioural therapies

Medication may also be necessary for some children as we work on the root causes and eventually adopt a drug-free approach where we can.

Dietary Changes

- Identify allergies or sensitivities. This is done through either observation or through immunoglobulin E (IgE) or immunoglobulin G (IgG) blood tests. Removing these antibodies reduces gut wall irritation and reduces stress in the overburdened immune system. Often a low-phenol/salicylate or a low-oxalate diet may be necessary. Additionally, most children will benefit from a gluten and casein-free (GFCF) diet. This is because these two proteins, when broken down, have a similar structure to opiates. In individuals with an inflamed gut, these may cause "zoning out", repetitive behaviour, sleep disturbances, constipation, and high pain tolerance.

- **Improve the health of the digestive tract.** Reduce inflammation and balance the bacteria (reducing dysbiosis) as there may be more opportunistic microbes from candida, strep, staph and less of the good bacteria such as *Lactobacilli* and *Bifidobacteria* in these individuals. These opportunistic microbes may cause neurological changes. For example, *Candida spp* produces alcohol from any sugar or carbohydrate, which affects brain health. *Streptococcus* are often elevated in autism, ADHD, and OCD cases. The strep produces toxins that may cause the symptoms of these disorders. Paediatric autoimmune neuropsychiatric disorders (PANDAS) are associated with streptococcal infections.

- **Address methylation, detoxification, oxidation, autoimmunity, and genetics.** Your health practitioner will discuss with you how he or she may detect methylation, pyrroluria, heavy metal toxicity, and more. These conditions can then be treated. Testing may include

- Urinary kryptopyrroles to determine pyrroluria (which results in B6 and zinc deficiencies)

- Blood tests: plasma zinc and serum copper, iron studies, full blood count, vitamin D, folate/ B12, serum creatinine, homocysteine and streptococcal serology (if PANDAS is suspected) and other tests

- Heavy metal toxicity

- Genetic testing

- Stool testing

Treatment of the root causes and symptoms

Dietary changes may include a specific ADHD/autism diet. More likely, you will address your child's individual needs. Often sugar and artificial additives are the first to be eliminated. Then any known allergens are eliminated, followed by processed flour products. Depending on the individual's symptoms, we may consider low casein, gluten, phenol, oxalate, or salicylate diets.

Herbal medicines may be prescribed, and nutritional medicines may be used to:

- Balance biochemistry and address deficiencies

- Provide nutrients for growth and development

- Boost immunity

- Reduce inflammation

- Reduce oxidative damage

Specific nutrient requirements (prescribed once we know which are necessary or beneficial) may include zinc, probiotics, cod liver oil (with vitamins A and D), P5P, vitamin C, calcium and magnesium, and others.

ADHD and EMFs exacerbated by mobile devices

Many studies have found a strong correlation between ADHD and EMF and radiation exposure. Limiting screen and phone time and using EMF-blocking devices may be useful.

ADHD Learning

Last but not least, understanding that different children have different ways of learning is so important. Most children (and adults) who have ADHD are kinesthetic learners. That means they're hands-on learners. So know that, if you try and put them in a classroom and tell them to sit there and not move for eight hours straight, that isn't natural for them.

That is not to say that, by following these tips, they can't do that — I'm sure they can — but finding a school system in which teachers understand kinesthetic learning, are patient, and can be hands-on is one of the best ways of supporting children who struggle with ADHD.

THE HEALTHY EATING SHOPPING LIST

Fruits and vegetables	Others
Choose seasonal fruits and vegetables where possible.	Powdered dried ginger
Broccoli, cabbage, onions, green leafy vegetables, potatoes, carrots	Herbs and spices (fresh or dried)—garlic, ginger, coriander, lemon pepper, etc. for flavouring foods
Salad vegetables	Tofu (made from soy and a nutritious protein alternative)
Frozen berries (for smoothies)	
Dried apricots and raisins	Marmite or Vegemite—great spreads that can also be used to flavour food
Fresh lemons for drinks and food flavouring	Lite or gluten-free soy sauce for cooking (use in moderation)

Grains and pulses	Nuts and seeds
Wholemeal bread, spelt or potato bread, millet or wholemeal oats (for porridge or muesli)	Sunflower and pumpkin seeds
Linseed or LSA (ground linseed, sunflower seeds, and almonds) to add to porridge, smoothies, fruit, or muesli (high omega three / good oils content).	Walnuts, almonds, and brazil nuts Tahini paste
Brown rice, noodles	
Lentils, kidney, and cannellini beans	
Tinned or dried beans— kidney, butter beans	
Hummus (made from chickpeas)	
Rice crackers	
Eggs	**Drinks**
Organic if possible	Green or light-blue top milk, mineral water, herbal teas
	Rice, almond, oat, or coconut milk (fortified varieties)
	Vegetable juice
	Apple juice (unsweetened)

Meats, poultry and fish	Oils and fats
Salmon, tuna, anchovies, or any other fish, lean red meats, poultry (skin off)	Flaxseed oil
	Extra virgin olive oil
	Olive- or avocado-based spread or fresh avocado
	Butter for cooking

Appendix 2

BASIC HEALTH SUPPLEMENT SUPPORT FOR YOUR KIDS

For Immunity: For eczema, upper respiratory complaints, allergy, hay fever, sinusitis, ear infections, coughs and colds:

- Probiotics

- Zinc

- Vitamins C, A, and D

- Essential oils: eucalyptus, oregano, tea tree

- Herbs: echinacea, eyebright, olive leaf, liquorice, marshmallow

For gut health (gut flora disruption, diarrhoea, constipation, IBS, poor digestive function):

- Omega 3 fish oils

- Probiotics

- Glutamine

- Zinc

- Essential oils: peppermint

- Herbs: slippery elm, marshmallow, liquorice, milk thistle

For mental and emotional health (learning, memory, concentration, cognitive development, nervous system function, insomnia, stress and anxiety):

- Omega 3 fish oils

- Magnesium (plus Epsom salts in the bath)

- Probiotics

- Vitamin D3 (more in winter than summer)

- Essential oil: lavender

- Herbs: chamomile, passionflower

Basics to have at home

- Cod liver of fish oil capsules

- Probiotics

- Vitamin C and zinc in winter

- Therapeutic essential oils: tea tree, lavender, and peppermint

- Homeopathics: arnica, aconite, belladonna, and Rescue Remedy® (a commercial blend of flower essences)

- Bach flower remedies.

Take care to supplement under the guidance of a health professional. Always aim to buy the highest-quality supplements you can afford. "Health professional only" supplements tend to be the best.

RESOURCES AND RESEARCH

This book is based on evidence from research published in various journals, knowledge gained from thousands of years of traditional use, or my personal experience gained in clinic over the last thirty years.

I have provided a few resources and journal articles to back up the information in the book, but I also encourage you to do your own research and make your own empowered decisions about how you wish to manage the health of your children.

Check out my website, www.sheenahendonhealth.co.nz, for more interesting articles. Join my Facebook community https://www.facebook.com/SheenaHendonHealth/ or feel free to email me at sheena@sheenahendonhealth, and I will endeavour to answer any questions.

Resources

Bartkowiak, J. (2010). NLP for Children. London, UK: MX Publishing.

Bone, Kerry. (2003). *A Clinical Guide to Blending Liquid Herbs: Herbal Formulations for the Individual Patient*. Edinburgh: Churchill Livingstone.

Braun, L. and M. Cohen. (2010). *Herbs and Natural Supplements: An Evidence-Based Guide* (3rd ed.). Sydney, Australia: Churchill Livingstone.

Dacey, J. (2016). *Your Anxious Child: How Parents and Teachers Can Relieve Anxiety in Children* (2nd edition). Published online. John Wiley & Sons, Ltd.

Kiwi Families. (2019). *First Day of Primary School Checklist.* Retrieved from https://www.kiwifamilies.co.nz/articles/first-day-of-primary-school-checklist/.

Lipski, E. (2012). *Digestive Wellness: Strengthen the Immune System and Prevent Disease Through Healthy Digestion* (4th ed.). New York, NY: McGraw-Hill.

Murray, M., J. Pizzorno, and L. Pizzorno. (2005). *The Encyclopedia of Healing Foods.* New York, NY: Atria Books.

Murray, M., J. Pizzorno, and L. Pizzorno. (2005). *The Encyclopedia of Natural Medicine (3rd ed).* New York, NY: Atria Books.

Nutrition Foundation (2019, September). Healthy Eating. Children. Retrieved from https://nutritionfoundation.org.nz/healthy-eating/children.

Santich, R. (2008). *Phytotherapy Essentials—Healthy Children: Optimizing Children's Health with Herbs.* Queensland, Australia: Phytotherapy Press.

Sarris, J., and J. Wardle. (2010). *Clinical Naturopathy: An Evidence-Based Guide to Practice.* Sydney, Australia: Churchill Livingstone Elsevier.

World Health Authority (WHO). (2019). *WHO Nutrition Health Topics.* Geneva, Switzerland. WHO Press. Retrieved from https://www.who.int/nutrition/topics/en/.

Research

Adolphus, K., C. L. Lawton, C. L. Champ, and L. Dye. (2016). "The Effects of Breakfast and Breakfast Composition on Cognition in Children and Adolescents: A Systematic Review." *Advances in Nutrition* (Bethesda, Maryland), 7(3), 590S–612S. doi:10.3945/an.115.010256.

Ahmadipour, S. (2017). "Phytotherapy for children's nocturnal enuresis." *Journal of Medical and Biomedical Sciences* (2017) 6(3), 23–29.

Becknell, B., M. Schober, L. Korbel, and J. D. Spencer. (2015). "The diagnosis, evaluation and treatment of acute and recurrent pediatric urinary tract infections." *Expert Review of Anti-infective Therapy*, 13(1), 81–90. doi:10.1586/14787210.2015.986097.

Besedovsky, L., T. Lange, and J. Born. (2012). "Sleep and immune function." *Pflugers Archiv: European Journal of Physiology*, 463(1), 121–137. doi:10.1007/s00424-011-1044-0.

Bhesania, N., and G. Cresci. (2017). "A nutritional approach for managing irritable bowel syndrome." *Current Opinion in Pediatrics*, 29(5), 584–591. doi:10.1097/MOP.0000000000000536.

Bleich, S. N., and K. A. Vercammen. (2018). "The negative impact of sugar-sweetened beverages on children's health: an update of the literature." *BMC Obesity*, 5, 6. doi:10.1186/s40608-017-0178-9.

Cruchet, S., Y. Lucero, and V. Cornejo. "Truths, Myths and Needs of Special Diets: Attention-Deficit/Hyperactivity Disorder, Autism, Non-Celiac Gluten Sensitivity, and Vegetarianism." *Annals of Nutrition Metabolism* 2016;68(suppl 1):42-50. doi: 10.1159/000445393.

Dimov, Stefanie, Lisa K. Mundy, Jordana K. Bayer, Felice N. Jacka, Louise Canterford, and George C. Patton. (2019). "Diet quality and mental health problems in late childhood," *Nutritional Neuroscience*, DOI: 10.1080/1028415X.2019.1592288.

Flores-Mireles, A. L., J. N. Walker, M. Caparon, and S. J. Hultgren. (2015). "Urinary tract infections: epidemiology, mechanisms of infection and treatment options." *Nature reviews. Microbiology*, 13(5), 269–284. doi:10.1038/nrmicro3432.

Forchielli, M., and W. Walker. (2005). "The role of gut-associated lymphoid tissues and mucosal defence." *British Journal of Nutrition*, 93(S1), S41-S48. doi:10.1079/BJN20041356.

Friedman, N. D., E. Temkin, and Y. Carmeli. (2018). "The negative impact of antibiotic resistance." *Clinical Microbiology and Infection*. Volume 22, Issue 5, 416—422. Retrieved from https://www.clinicalmicrobiologyandinfection.com/article/S1198-743X(15)01028-9/fulltext.

Gabriel, M. (2018). "The hygiene hypothesis at a glance: Early exposures, immune mechanism and novel therapies." *Acta Tropica*, Volume 188, Pages 16-26, ISSN 0001-706X, https://doi.org/10.1016/j.actatropica.2018.08.032. Retrieved from http://www.sciencedirect.com/science/article/pii/S0001706X18306880.

Hadhazy, Adam. (2010). "Think Twice: How the Gut's 'Second Brain' Influences Mood and Well-Being." *Scientific American*. http://www.scientificamerican.com/article/gut-second-brain/.

Koplin J. J., E. N. Mills, and K. J. Allen. "Epidemiology of food allergy and food-induced anaphylaxis: is there really a Western world epidemic?" *Current Opinion in Allergy and Clinical Immunology*. 2015;15(5):409-416.

Kessel, E. M., A. E. Allmann, B. L. Goldstein, M. Finsaas, L. R. Dougherty, S. J. Bufferd, G. A. Carlson, and D. N. Klein. (2017).

"Predictors and Outcomes of Childhood Primary Enuresis." *Journal of the American Academy of Child and Adolescent Psychiatry*, 56(3), 250–257. doi:10.1016/j.jaac.2016.12.007.

Lee, S. J. (2018). "Recent advances in managing lower urinary tract infections." *F1000Research*, 7, F1000 Faculty Rev-1964. doi:10.12688/f1000research.16245.1.

Martins, M., and F. Abecasis. (2016), "Healthcare professionals approach paediatric fever in significantly different ways and fever phobia is not just limited to parents." *Acta Paediatr*, 105: 829-833. doi:10.1111/apa.13406.

Mayo Clinic. "Chronic stress puts your health at risk." Retrieved from http://www.mayoclinic.org/healthy-living/stress-management/in-depth/stress/art-20046037. Accessed September 9, 2019.

Mitre E., A. Susi, L. E. Kropp, D. J. Schwartz, G. H. Gorman, and C. M. Nylund. "Association Between Use of Acid-Suppressive Medications and Antibiotics During Infancy and Allergic Diseases in Early Childhood." *JAMA Pediatrics*. Published online June 01, 2018172(6):e180315. doi:10.1001/jamapediatrics.2018.0315.

National Institute of Diabetes and Digestive and Kidney Diseases. "Your Digestive System and How it Works." http://www.niddk.nih.gov/health-information/health-topics/Anatomy/your-digestive-system/Pages/anatomy.aspx.

New Zealand Ministry of Health. (2012). "Food and Nutrition Guidelines for Healthy Children and Young People (Aged 2–18 years): A background paper"—Revised February 2015. Wellington: Ministry of Health.

Nieman, D. C., and L. M. Wentz. (2019). "The compelling link between physical activity and the body's defense system.' *Journal of sport and health science, 8*(3), 201–217. doi:10.1016/j.jshs.2018.09.009.

Rodriguez, D. (2019). "Small Intestinal Bacterial Overgrowth in Children: A State-of-the-Art Review." *Frontiers in Pediatrics*, Volume 7, pages 363. Retrieved from https://www.frontiersin.org/article/10.3389/fped.2019.00363.

Roszkowska, A., M. Pawlicka, A. Mroczek, k. Bałabuszek, and B. Nieradko-Iwanicka. (2019). "Non-Celiac Gluten Sensitivity: A Review." *Medicina (Kaunas, Lithuania)*, 55(6), 222. doi:10.3390/medicina55060222.

Samuel, T. M., K. Musa-Veloso, M. Ho, C. Venditti, and Y. Shahkhalili-Dulloo. (2018). "A Narrative Review of Childhood Picky Eating and Its Relationship to Food Intakes, Nutritional Status, and Growth." *Nutrients*, 10(12), 1992. doi:10.3390/nu10121992.

Schmeer, K. K., J. L. Ford, and C. R. Browning. (2018). "Early childhood family instability and immune system dysregulation in adolescence." *Psychoneuroendocrinology* 102: 189-195.

Sicherer, Scott H. et al. (2018). "Food allergy: A review and update on epidemiology, pathogenesis, diagnosis, prevention, and management." *Journal of Allergy and Clinical Immunology*, Volume 141, Issue 1, 41—58.

Simon, A. K., G. A. Hollander, and A. McMichael. (2015). "Evolution of the immune system in humans from infancy to old age." *Proceedings. Biological Sciences*, 282(1821), 20143085. doi:10.1098/rspb.2014.3085.

Singh, A., C. J. Yeh, N. Verma, and A. K. Das. (2015). "Overview of Attention Deficit Hyperactivity Disorder in Young Children." *Health Psychology Research*, 3(2), 2115. doi:10.4081/hpr.2015.2115.

Tamburini, S., N. Shen, H. Wu, and J. C. Clemente. (2016). "The microbiome in early life: implications for health outcomes." *Nature Medicine*, 22, 713-722.

Vighi G., F. Marcucci, L. Sensi, G. di Cara, and F. Frati. (2018). "Allergy and the gastrointestinal system." *Clinical and Experimental. Immunology.* 2008;153:3–6. doi: 10.1111/j.1365-2249.03713.x. http://www.ncbi.nlm.nih.gov/pmc/articles/PMC2515351/.

Williams, C. L., M. Bollella, and E. L. Wynder. "A new recommendation for dietary fiber in childhood." *Pediatrics* 1995;96:985–8.

Zhuang, L., H. Chen, S. Zhang, J. Zhuang, Q. Li, and Z. Feng. (2019). "Intestinal Microbiota in Early Life and Its Implications on Childhood Health." *Genomics, Proteomics & Bioinformatics*, 17(1), 13–25. doi:10.1016/j.gpb.2018.10.002.

ABOUT SHEENA HENDON

My mission is to educate, share, and motivate people to think, feel, be, and look as healthy and well as possible.
—Sheena Hendon

Born and educated in the UK, Sheena Hendon studied at Kings College University, London, UK, where she completed a Bachelor of Science Honours degree in nutrition and dietetics.

She was awarded a scholarship to Dunedin University, New Zealand, when she completed her degree, and that was when she fell in love with the country. She went back to the UK to complete her qualifications but returned to New Zealand over twenty-five years ago. Sheena is married to a Kiwi and has two gorgeous teenage boys.

Through further study in New Zealand, Sheena has become qualified in naturopathic and herbal medicine (Bachelor of Health Sciences with Distinction) and in nutrigenomics. She is a master neuro-linguistic programming (NLP) practitioner.

Sheena takes a holistic and natural approach to health and works with the mind and body to get some profound results. She works directly with her clients and also hosts empowering group seminars and workshops. She believes that both orthodox and complementary medicine have parts to play in a person's quest for health—neither has all the answers, but used together, they can provide incredible results.

Sheena set up and ran the well-regarded Auckland-based health clinic Elementa for eight years. Today she focuses on private child and adult consultations in New Zealand and overseas as well as running community and corporate health and wellness seminars and writing about health and wellness.

www.sheenahendonhealth.co.nz; https://www.facebook.com/Sheena HendonHealth/

Printed in the United States
By Bookmasters